# SpringerBriefs in Accounting

**Series editors**

Peter Schuster, Schmalkalden, Germany
Robert Luther, Bristol, UK

More information about this series at http://www.springer.com/series/11900

Sandro Brunelli

# Audit Reporting for Going Concern Uncertainty

Global Trends and the Case Study of Italy

 Springer

Sandro Brunelli
Department of Management and Law
University of Rome Tor Vergata
Rome
Italy

ISSN 2196-7873                    ISSN 2196-7881    (electronic)
SpringerBriefs in Accounting
ISBN 978-3-319-73045-5           ISBN 978-3-319-73046-2    (eBook)
https://doi.org/10.1007/978-3-319-73046-2

Library of Congress Control Number: 2017962049

Printed on acid-free paper

This Springer imprint is published by the registered company Springer International Publishing AG part of Springer Nature
The registered company address is: Gewerbestrasse 11, 6330 Cham, Switzerland

*To People Who Raised Me*

# Foreword

Transformation and uncertainty are the two main words used to describe the current economic environment. What was impossible and unpredictable just few years ago is now under the eyes of everyone.

The world is changing at the speed of light, much more rapidly than in the past. What next is almost impossible to predict.

Nowadays, a child has virtually the knowledge of the world in his palms but a Board may have troubles to understand the evolutions to come and making plans can be something like a guessing game. Especially when the firm's life is at stake and its continuity has a going concern as a risk.

At the same time, the long financial crisis has shaken business sectors globally and its end has been wrongly predicted many times along these years. Again, uncertainty becomes the lite motive of the business life, bankruptcies increase and the going concern issues became more difficult to predict.

The going concern represents one of the most important underlying assumptions for preparing financial statements and it is fundamental that stakeholders can trust that both Board of Directors and Auditors have and use all the possible instruments to properly address and communicate the ability of a company to continue its life in a sustainable way.

The role of the auditors is both difficult and fundamental in this environment and Prof. Sandro Brunelli offers us a ticket for an interesting global trip to understand how Audit Reporting for Going Concern Uncertainty is addressed in different jurisdictions and how it will change in the future to improve the financial reporting to benefit stakeholder' companies worldwide.

At the end of the journey, some open points remain to be addressed by future studies. For instance, in terms of impact and reaction of Going Concern Opinions on different stakeholders categories. This book gives the reader (graduate, scholars, regulators, auditors) a complete picture of the state of the art of this fundamental issue for financial reporting globally.

Rome, Italy

Giovanni Poggio
PWC Italy Partner

# Preface

The interest in writing a book related to Audit Reporting for Going Concern Uncertainty (GCU) has grown in me since the middle of 2016.

At that time, I started, with a colleague in Tor Vergata and the other two from other Roman universities, a wide research project aimed at feeding the debate about the investor' reaction to and perception of the so-called Going Concern Opinions (GCOs). I discovered a world in terms of literature, regulation, auditing and accounting practices, approaches and ways to detect the effects of GCOs on the entire stakeholder plethora. Thus, even though research papers are welcome, an in-depth analysis in the form of a dedicated book seems suitable as well.

Currently, the picture of Audit Reporting for GCU is huge and includes plenty of studies. In the USA, the Public Company Accounting Oversight Board (PCAOB), the auditing standards setter, has recently proposed the Going Concern (GC) as a next action under consideration; in Europe, the International Auditing and Assurance Standards Board (IAASB) has made an extensive revision of several auditing standards including the International Auditing Standards (ISA) 570—Going Concern.

At the same time, the GC represents worldwide an important underlying assumption for the preparation of financial statements—perhaps, the most important.

The Financial Accounting Standards Board (FASB) issued on 27 August 2014, the 'Accounting Standards Update No. 2014–15, *Disclosure of Uncertainties about an Entity's Ability to Continue as a Going Concern'*. It constitutes an amendment to the standard provided by the FASB, in November 1978, 'Original Pronouncements as amended, *Statement of Financial Accounting Concepts No.1*. In the European context, the International Accounting Standards Board (IASB) did not provide a specific standard for GC because of its explicit nature of underlying assumption within the Conceptual Framework. Indeed, GC is treated only in the *'Conceptual Framework for Financial Reporting'*, for which the last update was released in 2010 even though the framework, for other reasons, is currently under review. In brief, we are assisting to a reverse evidence for what concerns the GC and its links with accounting and auditing standards: On one hand, the 'auditing regulation' has been updated and reinforced on the European side; on the other hand, the 'accounting regulation' has been updated and reinforced on the American side. Thus, with regard to GC updating, PCAOB is a follower of the IAASB and IASB is a follower of the FASB. Above all, one question arises: Is it right to talk about leaders and followers in enhancing the overall quality of financial reporting worldwide? Obviously, the answer is no. However, more than this, it is interesting to investigate reasons behind these reversals and how, by also taking into account evidence from other jurisdictions, Audit Reporting for GCU will be addressed in the next years with the aim of enhancing the financial reporting system's reliability and usefulness for stakeholders.

This book is an attempt to outline the state of the art, by reviewing the main studies in this specific area using a narrative approach and providing some interesting empirical evidence from the Italian Stock Market by drawing out how investors react over time to GCOs. The aim is to enhance the quality of the debate by joining academic literature, standard setters' behaviours and empirical evidence, and taking into account the well-known existing international differences in financial reporting.

The book is divided into four chapters:

- Chapter 1 has a twofold aim: First, it simply reviews GC as an underlying assumption for the preparation of financial statements. It outlines GC's history in the accounting standards and how it is currently considered in the FASB and IASB accounting standards. Second, the same reasoning will be referred to the auditing field addressing how auditors in PCAOB and IAASB environments should verify the GC's presence in financial statements and what they outline as regards the audit report. In addition, accounting and auditing regulation insights related to GC in other jurisdictions will be shortly touched upon.
- Chapter 2 covers the heart of the issue. Starting from the seminal work led in the USA by Carson et al. (2013), the chapter reviews, with a narrative analytical approach, the debate related to Audit Reporting for GCU worldwide. In this regard, I decided to adopt for the same categorization as Carson et al. Thus, the researches on the theme will be reviewed by treating separately the determinants, accuracy and consequences of GCOs. Studies conducted in the USA, Europe and the rest of the world will be reviewed separately.
- Chapter 3 enriches the work with interesting empirical evidence from the Italian Stock Market. To this end, I will show how, in the period from 2008–2014, alongside the financial crisis, Italian investors reacted to GCOs, using the Event Study Methodology (ES). The results will be interpreted under different investigation profiles.
- Chapter 4, recovering the evidence found in the previous chapters, concludes the book by looking at a series of open issues, such as:

  – the reflections of GCOs in the light of agency theory;
  – how to read auditing rules for GCU and investors' reactions in the light of different country culture types deriving from international differences in financial reporting;

- Possible future Italian investors' behaviours, since novelties for periods ending on or after 15 December 2016 of several ISAs (above all the ISA 570 revised) foster, more than in the past, the release of a GCO;
- Whether and how auditing standard setters will implement fine-tuning actions or update auditing standards related to GCU;
- How scholars will feed the debate of Audit Reporting for GCU.

The reading of this book should be suitable for:

1. Graduates, to go into more depth in their study of auditing and financial reporting as a whole. Mainly for courses included in Master's of Science in Business Administration (or strictly related Master's programmes);
2. Scholars active in research projects in the field: First, to provide a structured general framework on audit reporting for GCU; second, to suggest future research pathways;
3. Regulators, I mainly refer to auditing standards setters and to have an overview of the state of the art worldwide;
4. Auditors, to enrich and enhance the debate around the issue, to foster an improvement of their internal procedure for releasing, or not, a GCO and, more in depth, to understand the importance of GCOs for stakeholders.

Rome, Italy                                                                               Sandro Brunelli

# Contents

# Chapter 1
# The Firm' Going Concern in the Contemporary Era

**Abstract** This chapter is aimed at reviewing the going concern (GC) assumption evolution over time in the two main regulatory accounting and auditing settings: International Accounting Standards Board (IASB) and Financial Accounting Standards Board (FASB) as regards the accounting standard setters, and International Auditing and Assurance Standards Board (IAASB) and Public Company Accounting Oversight Board (PCAOB) as regards the auditing standard setters. Addressing the GC evolution is prodromic to go further in depth on the academic debate about the relevance that GC assumption has throughout the financial reporting process: from the preparation of financial statements, to the audit process that ends with the issuance of the audit report. Lastly, some insights about the GC evolution in other countries' regulatory frameworks are provided (Australia, Canada, China, Japan, Russia and Singapore) in order to outline a worldwide representation of the GC auditing and accounting regulatory frameworks.

## 1.1 Study Motivation

The whole business sector is founded on the multiple interactions among the economic players, such as firms, investors and institutions. Above all, the dynamics of today's society are strictly associated with the transactions among them, incorporating wellness and the satisfaction of human needs. Therefore, it is important that companies, first, must survive as long as possible in a sustainable way, in order to meet the needs of people from elsewhere; indeed, business continuity constitutes a priority for a firm. However, for many years this has been taken for granted, even if financial problems were present and financial scandals have hit firms everywhere. In this sense, the auditor is a fundamentally professional figure charged with the duty of assessing the condition on which firms plan to continue to operate. For a long time, there was evident confusion on what the precise role of the auditor is within the financial environment. Many researches have drawn very different

S. Brunelli, *Audit Reporting for Going Concern Uncertainty*, SpringerBriefs in Accounting, https://doi.org/10.1007/978-3-319-73046-2_1

conclusions on this topic. After a very long period characterized by the lack of proper methods and techniques to be applied in detecting misstatements, clear regulations and ethical behaviour of every economic player, and after a series of huge financial scandals, auditors have assumed an ever increasing power over the sorts of companies.

The audit report is the result of the audit process and it represents the most important link between auditors and stakeholders. The interest in this topic is growing, as demonstrated by the great number of researches in this area. Also the regulation side has been very active in fostering improvements to auditing standards. Recently, the International Auditing and Assurance Standards Board (IAASB) has been involved in an extensive revision of several important auditing standards. The revised versions of six existing standards (ISA 260, 570, 700, 705, 706 and 720) and the issuance of a new one (ISA 701, related to Communicating Key Audit Matters in the Independent Auditor's Report) are effective for audits of financial statements, for periods ending on or after 15th December, 2016. In this respect, also other national auditing standards setters have revised and/or amended their standards. Among the related issues, the GC uncertainty and financial distress deserves further investigation because of its growing relevance throughout the world. According to John (1993), "*a firm is in financial distress at a given point in time when the liquid assets of the firm are not sufficient to meet the current liquidity requirements of its hard contracts*". Alternatively, financial distress is defined as the act of filing a petition for bankruptcy (Zmijewski 1984). A firm is identified as bankrupt if it filed a bankruptcy petition during a period. According to the International Accounting Standards Board's (IASB) conceptual framework for financial reporting, the GC represents one of the most important underlying assumptions for preparing financial statements. Consequently, the GC is also relevant during the auditing process, concluding with an audit report containing an opinion on the financial statement prepared for external users.

Today ISAs are largely adopted across the world in their current form or in a very similar form. The other most influential standards setter, even though not an international standards setter, is the Public Company Accounting Oversight Board (PCAOB). It issues its own Auditing Standards (AS) and they are applied to USA firms but also, in a very close form, in other jurisdictions. The amendments to ISAs related to GC made by the IAASB have represented an additional starting point to discuss similar actions by the PCAOB. As a matter of fact, the GC is highlighted in the PCAOB standards setting agenda as a next action under consideration to be addressed in 2018.

As outlined, GC is one of the most important underlying assumptions for the preparation of financial statements for external users. Thus, it is regulated through accounting standards issued by the IASB, the FASB and other national accounting standards setters (IFRS 2017). In this regard, although this book is aimed at reviewing Audit Reporting for GCU, this chapter firstly provides a short discussion about the birth and evolution of accounting standards related to GC in the IASB and FASB environment. Then it will focus on the auditing side of the evolution in respect of GC. Lastly, accounting and auditing standards evolution will be reviewed in several other jurisdictions.

## 1.2   Going Concern in IASB and FASB Accounting Standards

The concept of GC is defined in paragraph 4.1 of the *Conceptual Framework for Financial Reporting*[1] (IFRS 2010):

> The financial statements are normally prepared on the assumption that an entity is a going concern and will continue in operation for the foreseeable future. Hence, it is assumed that the entity has neither the intention nor the need to liquidate or curtail materially the scale of its operations; if such intention or need exist, the financial statements may have to be prepared on a different basis and, if so, the basis used is disclosed.

Whereas, the rule governing GC appears in International Accounting Standard (IAS) 1, paragraph 25 (IFRS 2008):

> When preparing financial statements, management shall make an assessment of an entity's ability to continue as a going concern. An entity shall prepare financial statements on a going concern basis unless management either intends to liquidate the entity or to cease trading, or has no realistic alternative but to do so.

If a company uses the GC basis of accounting, then:

(1) It cannot avoid a transfer that could be avoided only by liquidating or ceasing operations; but

(2) it has the ability to avoid (so it does not have the liability for) a transfer that would be required only to entity on liquidation or cessation of trading.

Judgement is required from both managers and auditors as they consider all the information at hand about the future performance of the firm to assess the appropriateness of the GC assumption. The degree of their judgement depends on the specific facts or features of each case.

The information about the future shall cover a period of at least 12 months after the date of the publication of the financial statements. When the entity has enough liquidity and easy access to financial resources, the assessment of the GC assumption is almost straightforward without any detailed analysis. Otherwise, the management needs to consider a broad array of indexes concerning current and potential profitability, debit coverage plans and alternative financial resources.

---

[1]Hereafter "Framework" or "Conceptual Framework".

The intent of IAS 1 is therefore to determine the effective moment in which the company is no longer able to operate under the assumption of GC, in order to protect the residual corporate assets and settle them in liquidation terms. Likewise, if significant uncertainties arise (albeit in the presence of the GC assumption), the rule provides for adequate disclosure in the financial statements. The inadequacy of the GC, however, may occur at any time, regardless of the liquidation or ceasing of the company.

In the U.S. GAAP conceptual framework, not only standards can be identified, but also some basic concepts and conventions that are implicitly taken into account in the financial statements.

The preparation of Financial Statements lies in a series of assumptions. According to the FASB, they are: materiality, stable monetary unit, periodicity, reliability, and GC.

The GC assumption consists of the fact that an entity will persist indefinitely; it is also referred as the continuity convention. This concept implies that a company will use its existing resources, such as plant assets, in order to fulfil its general business needs.

All these resources are intended to contribute to the production process and produce future cash inflows, concurring to generate profit. If the ability of a company to continue as a GC is not ascertained, these resources are valued at the price at which they could be sold to real estate or equipment markets immediately.

The opposite view of the continuity assumption is an immediate liquidation assumption, by which a company calculates the value of all items on its statement of financial position. These values are based on the appropriate amounts computed with the assumption that the entity will be liquidated in a retail market within a few days or months. This approach to valuation is used only when the probability that the company will be liquidated is really high.

Historically, GC has been discussed widely by the IASB in its "Conceptual Framework", while the attention devoted to this topic by the FASB framework was negligible until 2004, when the Financial Accounting Standard Advisory Board (FASAC) noticed that:

> The IASB framework prominently features two underlying assumptions: the accruals basis and the going-concern basis. These are not listed as underlying assumptions in the FASB framework. However, accrual accounting and related concepts are discussed extensively. In contrast, the going-concern basis is mentioned in a footnote only. Those assumptions will be considered when related parts of the framework are considered (elements and measurement).

The footnote referred to is in the "Conceptual Statements" (FASB 1978), dating back to 1978, and states that:

> Investors and creditors ordinarily invest in or lend to enterprises that they expect to continue in operation—an expectation that is familiar to accountants as "the going concern" assumption. Information about the past is usually less useful in assessing prospects for an

enterprise's future if the enterprise is in liquidation or is expected to enter liquidation. Then, emphasis shifts from performance to liquidation of the enterprise's resources and obligations. The objectives of financial reporting do not necessarily change if an enterprise shifts from expected operation to expected liquidation, but the information that is relevant to those objectives, including measures of elements of financial statements, may change.

Today, the situation has changed completely, evidencing a great reversal in the consideration and legislative treatment of the GC: FASB created an entire standard (in the form of Accounting Standard Update, ASU) in 2014 (FASB 2014), while, in the IASB environment, perhaps because its nature of underlying assumption, GC is still largely addressed in the conceptual framework.

## 1.2.1   The "Accounting Standards Update No. 2014–15"

The FASB issued, on 27th August 2014, "Accounting Standards Update No. 2014–15, *Disclosure of Uncertainties about an Entity's Ability to Continue as a Going Concern*". It constitutes an amendment to the standard provided in FASB, November 1978, "Original Pronouncements as amended, *Statement of Financial Accounting Concepts No. 1*", Objectives of Financial Reporting by Business Enterprises, previously cited. Its requirements impose on management the duty of assessing a company's ability to survive as a GC. On this matter, managers are required to provide related footnote disclosures in the verification of some conditions stated, by law. Previously, U.S. GAAP provided minimum guidance related to GC, since financial reporting assumes only that an organization will continue to operate as a GC until the moment in which its liquidation becomes imminent.

In the liquidation circumstances, financial statements should be prepared according to the liquidation basis of accounting, which is regulated by ASC 205-30 —*Presentation of Financial Statements-Liquidation.*

In accordance with the update, disclosures are mandatory conditions are verified that give rise to substantial doubts about the possibility of the firm continuing as a GC within one year from the financial statement issuance date. Substantial doubt is defined as the probability arising from pre-existing conditions and events of not self-fulfilling the obligations that come due from one year, counting from that issuance. This new standard is applicable to all companies and is enforceable for the annual period ending after 15th December, 2016, and all annual and interim periods thereafter.

If conditions that give rise to substantial uncertainties are verified, managers are required to prepare financial statements under the GC basis of accounting, although it may be necessary to disclose some important information in the footnotes to let them provide a more complete and truthful image of the overall company's financial health. The new standard provides a harmonized guidance usable by any kind of organization in situation of distress in their GC disclosure, deleting the diversity that existed in practice before this ASU.

Attention to this issue was raised by the concerns of auditors on GC. Presently, U.S. auditing standards and federal securities law prescribe to auditors the obligation of assessing a company's ability to continue as a GC, and auditing standards entail auditors to take into account management's footnote disclosures in their opinions.

FASB realized this ASU to incorporate some of the principles of the current auditing standards, in order to harmonize the legislation upon both accounting and auditing in the USA.

The FASB update:

- requires an assessment of the GC by management for each annual and interim reporting periods;
- provides a definition of substantial doubt;
- sets the looking-forward period for one year from the financial statement issuance date as the attention period, which has to be considered by the management in their evaluation;
- asks for disclosure about substantial doubt.

In brief, following the new standard, the presence of substantial doubt about the ability of the firm to continue as a GC is the trigger event to outline additional information.

On the one hand, firms registered by the Security Exchange Commission (SEC), with interim reporting duties, are required to assess GC uncertainties quarterly; on the other, private entities are required to carry out the same evaluation on an annual basis, or more frequently if they issue interim financial statements that are prepared under U.S. GAAP.

The standard update specifies the aggregate conditions giving rise to substantial doubt on the probability that a company will be not capable of meeting its obligations as they become due within a one-year horizon following the financial statement's issuance date. FASB statedthat substantial doubt refers to the conditions for which a likelihood threshold higher than 70 or 80% approximately exists, but management still has to consider all relevant qualitative and quantitative information and make judgements.

Managerial GC evaluation should be built on the relevant conditions known and reasonably knowable at the issuance date, paying attention to the most updated information available before Financial Statements issuance, as well as the events following that date. Managers are also required, through reasonable effort, to identify conditions not readily known, but identifiable without undue cost.

Among the conditions considered by the management in order to assess the presence or absence of substantial doubt about the ability of the organization to survive as a GC, there are:

- company's current financial condition, as current liquidity;
- conditional and unconditional obligations which come due within one year;

- funds necessary to maintain operations taking into account the company's financial conditions, obligations and expected cash flows for the current period, with a one year time horizon;
- other conditions that could affect in a negative way the firm's ability to meet its obligations in the next year, such as:

  - negative financial trends, such as persisting huge losses, negative net working capital, or negative cash flows;
  - other indications of financial troubles, such as: loans unrepaid, credit rating shutdown, requests for new debt, recurring assets disposals;
  - internal matters, such as unfruitful bargaining with trade unions,, unprofitable long-term commitments, continuous add and drop production lines
  - external matters, huge amount of contingent liabilities and provisions, loss of important customers, intangible long lived assets deterioration.

Managers need to judge the relevant aggregated conditions and assess the probability and dimension of their possible effect on the company's ability to honour their financial duties coming due during the assessment period.

If, after the assessment, substantial doubt on GC definitely arises, the standard requires managers to consider their plans about the future and the way in which they will address the situation.

Management should principally pay attention to two fundamental factors concerning the information contained in the mitigating plans:

- the probability according to which the plans will be effectively implemented during the assessment period;
- the probability according to which the plans realized by management will effectively mitigate the conditions that gave rise to substantial doubt.

The standard indicates that the probability for a plan to be effectively implemented relies on the fact that management or the board of directors must have approved the plan within the financial statement issuance date. Management also bears the responsibility for further assessing those plans and the probability of effectively mitigating the adverse GC conditions. The assessment of the plans should be based on the expected magnitude and timing of the mitigating effect of its plans.

If the assessment gives positive results, indicating that the managerial plans are able to alleviate the substantial doubt, the ASU requires the provision of some disclosures regarding the underlying conditions for substantial doubt and, consequently, the management's plans.

Only when the assessment gives negative results, and if substantial doubt remains uninfluenced by the management's plans, is it mandatory for the standard to provide a statement that declares there is substantial doubt about the company's ability to continue as a concern.

As regards the plans that are capable of influencing the conditions that make substantial doubts exist, the legislator provides some useful examples in order to identify the kinds of information managers are required to take into account in their evaluation, according to their likelihood of realization:

- plans to dispose of assets or businesses according to the marketability of the items;
- plans to take credit from outside or to modify debt through restructuring;
- plans to reduce or delay expenditures;
- plans to increase equity from ownership as additional capital.

Special attention should be reserved on analyzing the plans that are intended to liquidate the company. They should not be considered in the assessment of the plans for their mitigating effects on the conditions that influence substantial doubt about future business continuity, since they are contradictory by definition.

Explicit disclosures are mandatory only in the situation in which there exist conditions that give rise to substantial doubt, whether the substantial doubt is mitigated or not by managerial plans' actions.

No other kinds of disclosures are required specific to GCU assessment if substantial doubt is not detected by management.

In the occurrence of a situation in which substantial doubt is alleviated by management's plans, three kinds of disclosures are mandatorily required in the financial statements or footnotes:

- conditions giving rise to substantial doubt about the ability of the company to respect its obligations as they come due within one year from the financial statement issuance date;
- evaluation of the company's management of the relevance of these concerns;
- assessment of the managerial plans intended to mitigate substantial doubt.

In the occurrence of a situation in which substantial doubt is *not* alleviated by management's plans, disclosures are required in order to let all kinds of stakeholders, but especially investors, understand some information regarding the underlying conditions, such as:

- a statement explaining that there exists substantial doubt about the company's ability to continue its operations as a GC with a one year time horizon;
- the underlying conditions that make substantial doubt arise;
- managerial assessment of the seriousness of the conditions;
- plans implemented by management that were intended but were not able to alleviate the negative conditions.

Security Exchange Commission (SEC) filers are allowed to use Management Discussion and Analysis (MD&A, also known as Management Commentary) to expand and clarify footnote disclosures through the provision of additional context about the causes and effects of GC uncertainties. In the following reporting periods, either annual or interim ones, management is still required to provide disclosures on the situation in which substantial doubt continues to exist.

The nature of the disclosures should change in accordance with the availability of information about the financial situation of the company and the related management's implemented plans. Information about context and continuity should be added in order to provide investors with a clear as possible picture of the company's financial situation.

If substantial doubt is erased during the reporting period, the standard requires that the company mandatorily discloses both how the situation changed and the underlying conditions were improved.

Summing up the referred to updates, GC is now largely addressed on the accounting side with the purpose of fostering and in-depth control, also from auditors called to express an opinion on the overall fairness of the Financial Statements.

## 1.3  Going Concern in the Auditing Standards

Understanding the key issues which link the accounting and auditing fields is pivotal to have a critical overview of the focal point of our work.

The concept of GC is clearly defined by *International Standard on Auditing (ISA) 570* revised, which lists a series of events and circumstances that may cast substantial doubt on the appropriateness of the GC postulate. According to this standard, the auditor, in assessing the significance of uncertainty, shall take into account not only the potential effect, but also the probability that uncertain events will occur, determining misleads, because of its non-compliance with the accounting principles or because of the lack of a true and fair representation.

In particular, some financial indicators are pivotal for this acknowledgement:

- negative net equity or low or negative net working capital;
- loans at maturity and close to maturity without any possibilities to renew or to redempt in the short time; or huge amount of short-term loans used for financing non current assets;
- credit rating deterioration;
- persisting negative trends in profitability and solvency ratios;
- significant impairment losses on assets;
- discontinuity or lack of good dividens for shareholders;
- inability to raise money for new products or investments in long lived assets.

There can be also considered facts and events concerning the management, such as:

- loss of key managers without succeeding in replacing them;
- loss of significant market share, agreements or major suppliers;
- employees' internal disputes.

It is worth noting that this list is not exhaustive and the presence or absence of some of these items is not essential to indicate the existence of significant uncertainty. Although the GC is the basic principle for the preparation of the annual or periodic financial statements, its indication has hardly ever been subject to substantive verification; actually, management has always taken it for granted.

In this perspective, the elaboration of plans for the recovery of a "business crisis" is of great importance. Indeed, the main goal sought is the maintenance of the efficiency of the business system aimed at its continuation over time.

The recovery is achieved through a comprehensive restructuring of the company and interventions are different depending on the reasons that caused the crisis. The recovery of the production system requires different assessments regarding how the company will continue. All this can be achieved mainly through:

(1) the elaboration of a recovery and/or restructuring plan aimed at overcoming the causes of the crisis, having as its objectives the return to economic and financial equilibrium and the relaunch of the enterprise;
(2) the perpetuation of the business activity, also through the sale of the business or part of it.

In particular, a recovery plan is a document in which the strategy is drawn by management to return to the value of the enterprise before the crisis, or to the rebalancing of the economic and financial situation of the company. There are no legislative provisions governing its form and content. Therefore, it is necessary to reconsider the guidelines set out in the practice of the business plan.

## 1.3.1 The Evolution of the Going Concern in Different Auditing Regulatory Frameworks

The current economic and financial crisis has long discussed the topic of GC with more and more emphasis. It has become very relevant, both at a national and international level, and has recently seen the publication of documents by the IAASB (2015a, b). It has stressed their significance and advised on the implementation of a number of procedures, which include, inter alia, adequate disclosure in the footnotes and in-depth audits by the auditors.

On the other hand, various financial scandals that have come into public view (see Parmalat and Royal Ahold in Europe; Enron, Worldcom, Tyco, Lehman Brothers in the USA, etc.) in recent years, point to a relevant amount of companies presenting financial and economic imbalances as to compromise the same GC. Its nature, content and communicative value have long been discussed in the traditional auditing model. A major issue has been the lack of transparency in financial statements, auditors, and the audit. Consequently, substantial changes in the model have been suggested and, in some cases, implemented by the standards setter bodies.

These provisions could affect the nature of the audit and the auditor. Among the most famous national and international standards setters, IAASB, PCAOB, and the Financial Reporting Council (FRC) in the UK are engaged with the task of optimising the auditing system, taking into account users' needs. Therefore, they have tried to address some expected effects of proposed changes, particularly including the enhanced informativeness of the audit report and its clarity, and specific attention given to essential issues that come up during the audit.

## 1.3.2  ISAs Revision and Going Concern in the IAASB Environment

According to the International Standard on Auditing (ISA) 570, "under the going concern basis of accounting, the financial statements are prepared on the assumption that the entity (...) will continue its operations for the foreseeable future".[2]

It is worth remarking that some auditing reporting frameworks require an explicit paragraph which provides a proper evaluation of the firm's ability to keep on as a GC, whereas others do not mandate such a specific requirement. Generally, this evaluation includes a judgement, at a particular point in time, concerning the uncertain future outcome of events or conditions. It comprises an overview of the degree of uncertainty of the latter, the size and complexity of the entity and the nature and environment of its business. The responsibility of the auditors is to obtain enough audit evidence come to a conclusion about the appropriateness of the management's use of the GC basis of accounting and to determine whether there is material uncertainty of the ability of the firm to operate in the near future. Nevertheless, the auditors cannot predict such forthcoming events and conditions and consequently the GC, even if they have all the information at hand; this means that the absence of any references does not assure any guarantee for the GC assumption.

If the auditor certifies that the management's assessment of the GC is valid and there is no material uncertainty, a clean opinion is issued. But be aware that firms can receive a clean opinion and a GCO at the same time, as well. On the other hand, if the auditor finds material uncertainty or if there is express disclosure of it, a qualified opinion in the form of except for, adverse opinion or disclaimer of opinion is released. Once more, it is worthwhile noting that this could happen in relation to totally different grounds other than GC.

This distinction is essential to our knowledge, because a clean audit opinion with an emphasis of matter paragraph related to GC can be easily misled with a modified audit opinion and vice versa.

The topic of GC has been of growing interest in light of the global financial crisis. Stakeholders, such as investors, creditors, suppliers, banks, and Government

---

[2]Paragraph 2.

authorities, have called for a rising focus on GC matters by management and auditors. That is why the International Auditing and Assurance Standards Board (IAASB) is working on this issue in its position of international auditing standards setter. However, many stakeholders, together with the members of the international regulatory community, believe that a more holistic approach to GC is necessary. Feedback to the IAASB has shed light on accounting issues, comprising a certain degree of misunderstanding of some concepts, for which supplementary explanation and regulation is needed to complement the IAASB's work on auditor reporting on GC. In particular, it is thought that such auditor reports can help financial users in making effective decisions and that audit reports do not constitute a guarantee for the future existence of the company,

As a result of these and other thoughtful claims, in 2015 the IAASB released six revised versions of existing standards (ISA 260, 570, 700, 705, 706 and 720) and the issuance of a new one (ISA 701, related to Communicating Key Audit Matters in the Independent Auditor's Report) came into force for audits of financial statements, for periods ending on or after 15th December, 2016.

The IAASB has tried to create an equilibrium between the entity's specific information about the auditor's findings and the need to have a standardized language describing how the auditor approaches a GC. In this regard, two of the mentioned revised ISAs deserve attention: ISA 700—"*Forming an Opinion and Reporting on Financial Statements*"—and ISA 570—"*Going Concern*".

The revision of ISA 570 has made the auditor's work effort relating to GC issue less complicated. In particular, the IAASB:

- has provided further guidance concerning the appropriate disclosures in case material uncertainty exists;
- has required the auditor to test the adequacy of disclosure in "close call" situations,[3] taking into account the applicable financial reporting framework. ISA 570 (revised) specifies the type of disclosures needed in this case, incorporating concepts from the International Financial Reporting Interpretations Committee's (IFRIC) Agenda Decision, as well as the FASB's work on GC.

The IAASB has also regulated that, in certain circumstances, matters relating to GC may be classified as Key Audit Matters (IAASB 2015c), because these could be a significant or difficult part of the auditor's judgement in forming an opinion on financial statements as a whole.[4]

The need for further implementation of the GC issue has also been emphasized by the Public Interest Oversight Board (PIOB), the global independent oversight

---

[3]Where there are events or situations that may cast significant doubt on the entity's ability to continue as a going concern, but management has mitigating plans, and the conclusion is that no material uncertainty exists.

[4]Auditors of financial statements of listed firms are compelled to communicate Key Audit Matters in accordance with the new ISA 701—*Communicating Key Audit Matters in the Independent Auditor's Report*. This communication is designed to provide transparency about matters that for the auditor are of greater importance in the financial statements of the current period.

body that ensures the activities of the IAASB follow due procedures and are responsive to public interest. The IAASB will continue to monitor any development relating to GC and, if appropriate, engage in discussion with IASB about this theme, in order for the standard-setter body to remain well-positioned.

The IAASB is willing to undertake a post-implementation review of the new and revised auditor reporting standards after two years from the effective date. This would include a discussion with the IASB and others on the results of the review and eventual consideration of whether further effort is needed in the area of auditor reporting on GC.

Additional information has been introduced by the revision of ISA 700. In particular, modifications to the structure of the auditor's report have occurred in order to emphasize the increasing relevance of the mandatory disclosure of GC. Consequently, new requirements have been added to that part of the report regarding "Responsibilities of Management for the Financial Statements": the importance of the auditor assessment of how management has approached the GC basis of accounting and evaluated the entity's ability to continue as a GC in the financial statements has been stressed, in addition to the former requirements. Following the previous reasoning made for the management, the auditor also has to consider the suitability of the use of managers of the GC basis of accounting and whether material misstatements are present.

Overall, the most significant modification concerns the validity of the auditor's report. In particular, ISA 700 (revised) states that the "reasonable assurance" obtained by the auditor's opinion of the statements is of high level, but it does not assure that an audit in compliance with ISAs will always spot some material misstatements in the future, if they exist. This basically sets apart some auditors' responsibilities in drawing an opinion on an entity, after the disclosure of GC in the audit report.

Returning the novelties of the ISA 570 (revised), it can be said that, in a certain sense, the GCO is close to being mandatory. A breakdown of the ISA 570 (revised) may justify this strong position, even though paragraph 7 of the standard states that:

> …the absence of any reference to a material uncertainty about the entity's ability to continue as a going concern in an auditor's report cannot be viewed as a guarantee as to the entity's ability to continue as a going concern.

In fact, it is quite hard to imagine, for audits of financial statements, for periods ending on or after 15th December, 2016, an audit report without any reference to GC. Figure 1.1, is a flow chart aimed at providing graphical evidence of the duties required by the auditor during the auditing process regarding the GC evaluation.

The additional procedures in the flow chart are not mandatory if the auditor concludes that there are no significant doubts that may be cast on the ability of the firm to continue its activity for the foreseeable future; on the other hand, even if the auditor concludes in that direction, he/she is free to point out his/her view about these remote doubts in the form of the emphasis of matter paragraph related to GC.

In conclusion, these new provisions have added more efficacy and fairness in the auditing field, by fine tuning the tasks of both auditors and managers during the

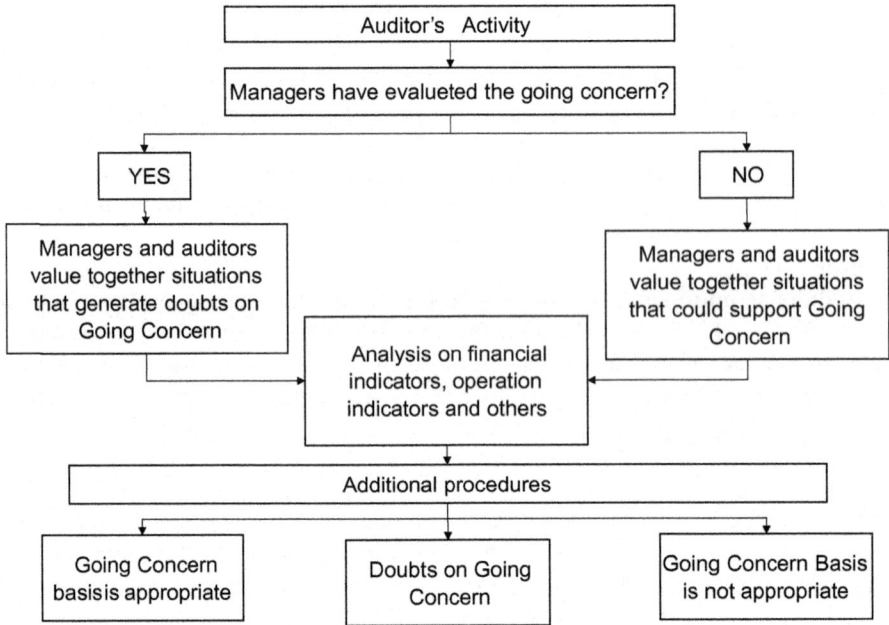

**Fig. 1.1** The auditor's duties in evaluating GC in financial statements. *Source* Author's elaboration

process in order to avoid enormous scandals in financial markets and, above all, to protect investors and stakeholders from being swindled.

### 1.3.3   Going Concern in the PCAOB Environment

In the USA, the organ devoted to the regulation of the audit profession, until the beginning of 21st century, was constituted by CPAs themselves, and associated into the American Institute of Certified Public Accountants (AICPA).

With regard to GC and its role in the Auditing Standards system, the AICPA legislated upon it in "AU Section 341", whose title is *"The Auditor's Consideration of an Entity's Ability to Continue as a Going Concern"* (AICPA 1989).

The pillars of the government regulation of the accounting profession in the US were provided by the Sarbanes-Oxley Act (SOX), promulgated in 2002.

The most important provisions were regarding the establishment of the Public Company Accounting Oversight Board (PCAOB), which was charged with the power of regulating many aspects of auditing and setting standards for audit reports' processing procedures.

The SOX Act forbade public accounting firms providing to the same clients, whose statements were under audit evaluation, from receiving other non-audit services (NAS), such as financial information systems design and implementation and internal audit outsourcing services.

To maintain the auditor's independence from the organizations receiving the audit service, the auditor firm, or coordinating partner, and the reviewing partner on an audit are bounded to rotate every five years, by law. The PCAOB has the duty to redact a register of all the accounting firms that offer audit services to the firms, whose stocks are publicly traded in an American Stock Exchange.

The same Act also regulated on corporate governance matters: every board of directors of publicly held companies is required to appoint an audit committee, made up of "independent" directors. Chief Executive Officers (CEOs) and Chief Financial Officers (CFOs) are expected to sign a special statement that declares their assumption of responsibility for the company's financial statements. Furthermore, the penalties applied to the management responsible for knowingly misreporting financial information, were increased.

Regardless of the government's interventions, through the institution of PCAOB and the promulgation of the SOX Act, the AICPA has maintained an important role in the accounting profession regulation. This association still has the duty to control the requirements necessary to have access to the accounting profession.

Today, the PCAOB is charged with the responsibility for issuing Generally Accepted Auditing Standards (GAAS) to make certain that all auditors properly apply the required technical knowledge. GAAS contain the fundamental and basic steps an auditor has to take in order to examine transactions and financial statements, issue an auditor's opinion and detect the errors or omissions in a company's financial statements.

The institution of the PCAOB, as a substitute for the AICPA for the regulation of the audit field, has generated a multisource system of auditing standards; that is why, in 2015 PCAOB published "PCAOB Release No. 2015-002, dated 31st March, 2015, known as *"Reorganization of PCAOB Auditing Standards and related amendments to PCAOB standards and rules"* (PCAOB 2015a).

The Objective of PCAOB has been to reorganize audting standards providing an integrated system of numbering. In this way, surfing among standards should be easier for users

Up to the 2015 PCAOB aforementioned reorganization, there were two kinds of standards, which were in force:

- those issued by the Auditing Standards Board (ASB), which was an organ of the American Institute of Certified Public Accountants (AICPA) and subsequently adopted by PCAOB o in April 2003;
- those issued by the PCAOB itself.

The PCAOB in April 2003 agreed to use standars issued up to that time. The Board decided to continue with the existing topic based organization and reference numbers ("AU sections") in the ASB's then-existing codification of its standards.

Up to that moment, the Board has issued 18 auditing standards (AS Nos. 1–18), which replaced 12 interim auditing standards and amended a vast part of the remaining interim auditing standards to different extents. The Board's auditing standards ended up being organized into two distinct numbering systems:

- the one used by the ASB for interim adopted auditing standards;
- the one created by the Board for its newly issued standards.

The Board undertook reorganization of the standards using a single, integrated numbering system and a topical structure that generally follows the flow of the audit process, to practically enhance their usability.

The PCAOB reorganized the standards substantially, in particular, the individual standards were grouped into these five topical categories:

- General Auditing Standards;
- Audit Procedures;
- Auditor Reporting—Standards for auditors' reports;
- Matters Relating to Filings Under Federal Securities Laws;
- Other Matters Associated with Audits.

The results of this reorganization were summed up in different tables that specified how the reorganization process modified the different articles.

With specific regard to the existing auditing standard related to GC, "AU Sect. 341" was renamed as "AS 2415" (PCAOB 2015b).

Although the title was modified to "*Consideration of an Entity's Ability to Continue as a Going Concern*", the substance and structure of the auditing standard remained unchanged.

In accordance with the standard, the auditor has the responsibility of evaluating the presence of substantial doubt about the entity's ability to continue as a GC for a reasonable period of time, within one year from financial statements' issuance.

The base of the assessment is composed of all the relevant conditions and events existing to the date of the auditor's report, that can form part of the auditor's knowledge. These pieces of information are gathered through auditing procedures planned and performed to achieve objectives related to management's declarations, contained in Financial Statements under auditing analysis.

GC valuation should be realized following the following steps:

- the auditor needs to evaluate whether, from the data gathered during the auditing process, substantial doubt could emerge. In that case, it is recommended to obtain additional information about the conditions and events that raised the substantial doubt, as well as the connected evidence;
- in the situation in which the auditor supposes substantial doubt exists, he or she is obliged to take two further steps:

  a. collect further information about managerial plans intended for those conditions or events;
  b. express a judgement on the likelihood that such plans can be effectively implemented.

- Subsequent to the evaluation of the plans that managers intend to implement, the auditor has the duty to conclude whether this substantial doubt is ascertained:

  a. if the result of the appraisal is positive and actually substantial doubt exists, the auditor has to consider the need for disclosure about the company's lack of ability to continue as a GC for a reasonable period of time;
  b. the auditor has to include an explanatory paragraph, which follows the opinion paragraph, in his audit report to reflect his or her conclusions;
  c. if the result of the analysis is negative and the auditor concludes that substantial doubt does not exist, the auditor should still consider the need for disclosure.

Even if the auditor has the duty to perform an audit following all the standards and procedures, he or she is not responsible for forecasting future conditions or events. As well as in ISA 570, the fact that substantial doubt is not present in the audit report of a company's financial statements does not provide assurance that the firm is completely free from any risk of ceasing to exist as a GC.

There is no need to design a special procedure for detecting conditions and events that make substantial doubt on the firm's continuity arise.

The regular auditing procedures that have to be followed to realize an audit report are sufficient to investigate GC. Some examples of procedures, according to the AS 2415, that may be useful to identify such conditions and events are:

- Analytical procedures;
- Review of subsequent events;
- Review of compliance with the terms of debt and loan agreements;
- Reading of minutes of meetings of stockholders, board of directors, and important committees of the board;
- Inquiry of an entity's legal counsel about litigation, claims, and assessments;
- Confirmation with related and third parties of the details of arrangements to provide or maintain financial support.

During the audit process, the auditor may find some conditions and events that, when considered overall, can give rise to substantial doubt.

Their significance will depend on the aggregated circumstances. Some examples of such conditions and events are:

- negative trends, such as recurring operating losses, working capital deficiencies, negative cash flows from operating activities, adverse key financial ratios;
- other indications of possible financial difficulties to mention a few: default on loan or similar agreements, arrearages in dividends, denial of usual trade credit from suppliers, restructuring of debt, non-compliance with statutory capital requirements, need to seek new sources or methods of financing or to dispose of substantial assets;
- internal matters, such as work stoppages or other labour difficulties, substantial dependence on the success of a particular project, uneconomic long-term commitments, need to significantly revise operation;
- external matters that have occurred, such as legal proceedings, legislation, or similar matters that might jeopardize an entity's ability to operate; loss of a key franchise, licence, or patent; loss of a principal customer or supplier; uninsured or underinsured catastrophe, such as a drought, earthquake, or flood.

If the presence of substantial doubt is ascertained, the auditor needs to consider management's plans intended to mitigate the effect of the events and conditions surrounding the substantial doubt regarding the company's GC.

The auditor should investigate these plans, evaluate their potential contribution to the mitigation of substantial doubt and assess the possibility to implement them effectively. The auditor's analysis should focus on:

- happened dispose of assets or the intention to do it;
- plans to borrow money or change debts maturity;
- plans to postpone or avoid expenditures;
- plans to increase equity.

After evaluating those elements in the managerial plans able to mitigate the negative effects, the auditor should perform auditing procedures in order to obtain evidence about them, such as the ability to secure financing or the disposal of assets.

If there exists some prospective financial information useful for the auditor's analysis, the auditor is entitled to ask management about its provision.

In accordance with AS 2415, The auditor should give particular attention to assumptions that are:

- material to the prospective financial information;
- especially sensitive or susceptible to change;
- inconsistent with historical trends.

It is fundamental for the auditor to consider the entity's knowledge, its business and its management and if the financial information is incomplete or misstated according to the factors known by the auditor, he/she should discuss them with management and eventually ask for the revision of prospective financial information.

If the auditor has ascertained the presence of substantial doubt, he/she should consider the possible effects on the financial statements and the adequacy of the related disclosure.

According to the standard, useful information that might be disclosed includes:

- pertinent conditions and events giving rise to the assessment of substantial doubt about the entity's ability to continue as a GC for a reasonable period of time;
- the possible effects of such conditions and events;
- management's evaluation of the significance of those conditions and events and any mitigating factors;
- possible discontinuance of operations;
- management's plans (including relevant prospective financial information);
- information about the recoverability or classification of recorded asset amounts, or the amounts or classification of liabilities.

In the circumstance in which substantial doubt is alleviated by management's plans, the auditor needs to consider the necessity for disclosure of the principal conditions and events that initially caused him or her to believe there was substantial doubt.

If after the conclusion of the analysis the auditor deduces that this doubt remains, he or she should add an explanatory paragraph to the opinion to show the conclusion.

The conclusion should be expressed in a standardized form, using the phrase "substantial doubt about the entity's ability to continue as a going concern", or similar phrasing including at least "substantial doubt" and "going concern".

If the company's disclosures with respect to GC are not enough according to auditors, a deviation from GAAP is verified. This may lead to either a qualified (except for) or an adverse opinion.

If substantial doubt is ascertained for the current period, this does not imply that it should also influence the judgements on financial statements dating back to previous periods, if presented together on a comparative basis.

On the other hand, if substantial doubt dating back to past periods has been erased in the present, it should not be specified in any additional explanatory paragraph.

Finally, if the existence of substantial doubt is ascertained, the auditor should document all of the following:

- the conditions or events that have putted in doubt the entity's ability to continue as a GC for a reasonable period of time;
- the elements of management's plans that the auditor considered to be particularly significant to overcoming the adverse effects of the conditions or events;
- the auditing procedures performed and evidence obtained to evaluate the significant elements of management's plans;
- the auditor's conclusion as to whether substantial doubt about the entity's ability to continue as a GC for a reasonable period of time remains or is alleviated. If substantial doubt remains, the auditor should also document the possible effects of the conditions or events on the financial statements and the adequacy of the related disclosures. If substantial doubt is alleviated, the auditor should also document the conclusion as to the need for disclosure of the principal conditions and events that initially caused him or her to believe there was substantial doubt;
- the auditor's conclusion as to whether he or she should include an explanatory paragraph in the audit report. If disclosures with respect to an entity's ability to continue as a GC are inadequate, the auditor should also document the conclusion as to whether to express a qualified or adverse opinion for the resultant departure from generally accepted accounting principles.

The standard has been in force since 1989. Summing up its provision, at first sight, it seems that there are not many differences when comparing it with the revised version of ISA 570. In spite of this, going a little more in depth, two main important differences emerge:

1. the new ISA 570 requires a specific in-depth procedure to detect if the GC basis is appropriate and test whether substantial doubts exist on the ability of the firm to perform for the foreseeable future. AS 2415 does not require specific

procedures, given the fact that, eventually, doubts may arise during other ordinary audit procedures;

2. the new ISA 570 does not call for a mandatory GCO only when there are no doubts even if it is in the availability of the auditor to say something about in the audit report; on the other hand, according to AS 2415, if there are no substantial doubts related to GCU the auditor should not argues nothing in the audit report in the form of additional explanatory paragraph, as well as in the case of substantial doubt dating back to past periods has been erased in the present.

From these two huge differences it is reasonable to think that the number of GCO of ISAs adopters will be greater, in the absence of AS 2415 similar updates, than the GAAS ones. That is why, according to the PCAOB Standard Setting Update released in the last quarter of 2016, the GC has a dedicated project on the research agenda to be addressed in the near future. In a subsequent Standard Setting Update (third quarter of 2017) the PCAOB is still considering the topic, but has decided to adopt a "wait and see" strategy, given the few times since the ASU (see para. 1.2.1) related to GC and the entrance in force of ISA 570 (revised) (even though in the update there are no references to the latter).

## 1.4 Going Concern in Accounting and Auditing Standards in Other Jurisdictions

In this paragraph I briefly point out the state of the art of GC in auditing and accounting standards in six important countries across the world: Australia, Canada, China, Japan, Russia and Singapore. As we will see, there are no great differences and the convergence pathway seems to be strongly consolidated. Notwithstanding, some differences remain, especially as regards the compulsoriness or not of the GCO.

*Australia*

In Australia the board that has the task of supervising auditors is the Australian Auditing and Assurance Standards Board (AUASB), which is an independent, statutory agency of the Australian Government. Since it is an autonomous board, there are also the Australian Standards on Auditing (ASA), and the auditing standard that refers to the GC is ASA 570 (AUASB 2015). As Australia is one of the developed countries, the standards they have are in conformity with the ISAs. Furthermore, in ASA 570 there are some additional paragraphs containing more information, or explanatory material on the Going Concern Standard. The extra paragraphs are the following:

- paragraph 3.1 refers to some specific requirements provided by the Corporations Act 2001;
- paragraph 13.1 states that auditors have to check the validity of management's GC assumption for the relevant period;

- paragraph 13.2 defines the relevant period to be almost 12 months from the date of the auditor's current report to the expected date of the auditor's next report for the following reporting period;
- paragraph 15.1 states the application material regarding the auditor's responsibility in the period beyond management's assessment.

Thanks to the revision of this standard and the AASB 101, which is the accounting standard on how financial statements should be properly prepared, including the management's assessment of the company's ability to continue operating, it is now the responsibility of the auditors to assess the GC ability of a company even if it is not stated by the management. These two provisions were made to avoid the self-fulfilling prophecy, a phenomenon that will be discussed later when considering the GCO as unavoidable doom for the company, which is that it will fail within 12 months of the auditors' report.

*Canada*

In Canada the two main organizations for auditing and accounting are the Chartered Professional Accountants of Canada (CPAC), which is a recent institution since it was created in 2011 as a result of a merger of the main accounting institutions previously present and the Auditing and Assurance Standard Board (AASB). The auditing standards are named Canadian Auditing Standards (CAS). The standard referring to the GC is CAS 570 (AASB 2009). This standard became effective on 14th December, 2010. It claims the auditors' responsibilities are to investigate and report whether a company can proceed as a GC, or report if there are some uncertainties about its ability to continue. In the history of CAS 570 there have been no amendments since its issuance. Recently there have been some proposals under consideration for an amendment of this standard, and a proposal for a new version of the Auditor Report, encompassing the changes that have been applied in the ISA 570 (revised). These changes have been accepted in April 2017, and will be effective for all the financial statements for periods ending on, or after, 15th December, 2018.

*China*

In China the two main controlling board on auditing and accounting standards are the Chinese Auditing Standards Board (CASB) and the Chinese Institute of Certified Public Accountants (CICPA). Starting from 2009, China decided to return to the global economy, so the authorities decided to converge their standards on IFRS. Starting from a period between the end of the 2010 and the beginning of 2011 up to 2012 has been the critical period for the convergence. Since they had problems with fraud and collusion by auditors and auditees, it is now imposed by the Government that special attention must be paid to the so-called Special Treatment (ST) companies whose business performance is bad or there have been serious accidents, which is a rule to reveal the investment risk of stock markets.

According to the State Certified Public Accountant Auditing Standards No. 1324 —Going Concern, it is within the accountants' financial responsibility to use the GC assumption in the preparation of financial statements with the management, and to provide a specification about this. CPAs carrying out the audit work need to pay particular attention and consider the matter.

In the aforementioned standard there are also the responsibilities and duties of the auditors.

In order to check whether the financial statements are well prepared by the management, auditors have to carry out the five following aspects of the work:

- in the implementation of the risk assessment process, consider whether there is the existence of any matter or circumstance that creates significant doubts in the audited statements or in the course of the entire audit.
- identify significant concerns that may be relevant to the GC ability of the audited firm on the matters, or circumstances, of interest. Implement additional audit procedures to determine whether there are such matters, or circumstances, related to a significant uncertainty.
- assess whether the financial statements have been fully disclosed and may result in a significant uncertainty about the matters or circumstances in which the GC ability of the audited firm has significant concerns.
- consider the impact of the audited firm's GC ability on the Auditor's Report.
- communicate with the audited firm's management (if applicable).

In China, as well as in Australia, it is compulsory to assess a judgement on the company's ability as a GC to avoid the self-fulfilling prophecy. Incidentally, even though they are still using their own standard for listed public companies, they are now introducing and experimenting with ISA 570.

*Japan*

In Japan the entity that has the task of supervising the accounting profession is the Japanese Institute of Certified Public Accountants (JICPA). In Japan even if IFRS are accepted, they still have their own system of standards, which for the auditing field is the Japanese Generally Accepted Auditing Standards (GAAS), which is an equivalent set of rules, and closer to the ISAs ones (JICPA 2013). In the revised version of the standards on auditing there is a subparagraph containing the GC opinion. The premise 6 about GCO has four main points about the responsibilities an auditor has while revising the management financial statements; these premises are:

1. although it is appropriate for the auditor's preparation of the financial statements on the premise of a GC, in cases where significant uncertainties concerning the premise of the continuity of a company are recognized, matters concerning the GC are appropriate for the financial statements. When announcing an unqualified appropriate opinion, judging what is previously stated, the auditor shall add to the audit report matters concerning the premise of the GC;
2. even if it is appropriate for the auditor's preparation of the financial statements on the premise of a GC, in cases where significant uncertainty regarding this premise is recognized, and the matters concerning the GC of company are appropriate for the financial statements, it must be stated. If it is judged that it is not fairly stated, the auditor shall either express a limited opinion attached with

exclusion paragraphs on the inappropriateness of the statement, or express an opinion that the financial statements are inappropriate, but isignificant uncertainty must always be stated;

3. if the auditor recognizes significant uncertainties regarding the premise of the GC when the management does not indicate an evaluation or countermeasure concerning the event or circumstance that causes a significant doubt,, it is necessary to judge the adequacy of the opinion in accordance with the case where an important audit procedure could not be carried out;

4. if management inappropriately prepares financial statements on the premise of a GC, the auditor must express an opinion that the financial statement's premises to be a GC are inappropriate, and there are no explanations for the uncertainty that has arisen.

*Russia*

In Russia, the federation overlooking the accountant professionals is the same Russian Government, which in the period prior to the convergence to the international standards, had its own regulations: Russian Accounting Standards (RAS). Now, instead, the Consolidated Financial Statements of listed companies must be in compliance with the IFRS, while, even if there has been the acceptance of the IFRS, other kinds of financial reports must be done in compliance with the old RAS.

In fact, in Russia there are two regulatory bodies, the first is the "Audit Chamber of Russia" administrated by the Russian government, and the second is "National Organization for Financial Accounting and Reporting Standards" an independent expert body advising the Russian Ministry of Finance regarding endorsement of IFRS in Russia.

Even if the IFRS have been accepted as those for listed companies, the standard related to the GC of non-listed companies is the Federal Rule (Standard) of Auditing Activity No. 11—"Applicability of the assumption of the continuity of the entity's activity" which established the requirement for the auditor to determine the ability of the entity being audited to continue its activities. GC assumption is the main principle in the preparation of financial statements. In accordance with the principle of assuming business continuity, it is usually assumed that the entity being audited will continue to exercise its financial and business activities during the 12 months of the year following the reporting year, and has no intention or need for liquidation, discontinuation of financial or business activities, or seeking protection from creditors. Assets and liabilities are accounted on the basis that the audited entity will be able to fulfil its obligations and realize its assets in the course of its activities. Audit of annual standalone statutory financial statements is compulsory for five categories of entities:

- joint Stock Companies.
- entities with securities listed on stock exchanges.
- banks, Credit Institutions and Insurance companies.
- entities with yearly revenues exceeding RUB 400 million (12.5 million USD) for the previous financial period.

- entities with total assets as at the preceding 31st December exceeding RUB 60 million (1.8 million USD)

*Singapore*

The body that has the task of supervising the professional accountants and auditors, in Singapore, is the Institute of Singapore Chartered Accountants (ISCA), while the Government based organization is the Accounting Standard Council (ASC) which recently has announced that all the Singapore Stock Exchange's listed companies will have to apply the IFRS from 2018 for the preparation of financial statements. The standard referring to the GC is SSA 570 (ISCA 2015) which has recently been revised, as it converges with the international one. In Singapore Financial Reporting Standard (FRS) 1, the one referred to in the preparation of the financial statement, there is a subparagraph referring to the GC principle, which requires the management to make specific assessments about the ability of the entity to continue as a GC. Usually the period considered for the GC principle is 12 months, but this could be extended for various reasons: usually a company that is profitable and has never had liquidity and/or solvency problems is part of those that have a period of 12 months.

# References

AASB (2009) Basis for conclusions Canadian Auditing Standard (CAS) 570, going concern. http://www.frascanada.ca/canadian-auditing-standards/resources/basis-for-conclusions/item30664.pdf

AICPA (1989) The auditor's consideration of an entity's ability to continue as a going concern. In: AU section 341. https://pcaobus.org/Standards/Auditing/Pages/AU341.aspx

AUASB (2015) Auditing standard ASA 570 going concern. http://www.auasb.gov.au/admin/file/content102/c3/ASA_570_2015.pdf

Deloitte (2013) Proposed narrow-focus amendment to IAS 1. https://www.iasplus.com/en/meeting-notes/iasb/2013/september/ias-1

FASAC (2004) Revisiting the FASB's conceptual framework. http://www.fasb.org/jsp/FASB/Document_C/DocumentPage&cid=1218220253854

FASB (1978) Statement of financial accounting concepts no. 1-objectives of financial reporting by business enterprises. In: Original Pronouncements as amended. http://www.fasb.org/resources/ccurl/816/894/aop_CON1.pdf

FASB (2014) Accounting standard update no. 2014-15, disclosure of uncertainties about an entity's ability to continue as a going concern. In: presentation of financial statements-going concern (Subtopic 205-40), Norwalk, Financial Accounting Series

IAASB (2015a) Auditor reporting on going concern. http://www.ifac.org/system/files/publications/files/Auditor-Reporting-Toolkit-Going-Concern.pdf

IAASB (2015b) International Standard on Auditing 570 (revised) going concern. http://www.ifac.org/system/files/publications/files/ISA-570-%28Revised%29.pdf

IAASB (2015c) International Standard on Auditing 701 communicating key audit matters in the independent auditor's report. http://www.ifac.org/system/files/publications/files/ISA-701_2.pdf

IFRS (2008) IAS 1–Presentation of financial statements. http://eifrs.ifrs.org/eifrs/bnstandards/en/IAS1.pdf

IFRS (2010) Conceptual framework for financial reporting. http://eifrs.ifrs.org/eifrs/bnstandards/en/framework.pdf

IFRS (2017) Convergence between IFRS standards and US GAAP, IFRS global standards for the world economy. http://www.ifrs.org/use-around-the-world/global-convergence/convergence-with-us-gaap/Pages/convergence-with-us-gaap.aspx

ISCA (2015) SSA 570 (revised)–Going concern. https://isca.org.sg/media/777078/ssa-570-revised-july-2015.pdf

JICPA (2013) Corporate disclosure in Japan–auditing. http://www.hp.jicpa.or.jp/english/about/publications/pdf/PUBLICATION-Auditing2013.pdf

John TA (1993) Accounting measures of corporate liquidity, leverage, and costs of financial distress. Financ Manag 22(3):91–100

PCAOB (2015a) PCAOB release No. 2015-002, reorganization of PCAOB auditing standards and related amendments to PCAOB standards and rules. https://pcaobus.org/Rulemaking/Docket040/Release_2015_002_Reorganization.pdf

PCAOB (2015b) AS 2415, consideration of an entity's ability to continue as a going concern. https://pcaobus.org/Standards/Auditing/Pages/AS2415.aspx

Zmijewski M (1984) Methodological issues related to the estimation of financial distress prediction models. J Account Res 22:59–82

# Chapter 2
# Audit Reporting for Going Concern Uncertainty: The Academic Debate

**Abstract** This chapter, using a narrative literature review, goes to the heart of the academic debate about Audit Reporting for Going Concern Uncertainty (GCU). With the aim of enhancing the understandability of the review, the studies are classified following the same, and well-known in the literature, categorization adopted by Carson et al. (2013). The purpose is to provide a worldwide faithful representation of what scholars have said over time with respect to Audit Reporting for GCU. This effort is necessary for a twofold reason: On the one hand it fills the gap of a missing worldwide representation of this richest debate; on the other, it helps scholars in understanding which are topics and subjects unexplored or underexplored that deserve academic and, not only, future engagement. Lastly, it provides auditors and regulators with a global synthesis about the determinants, accuracy and consequences of Going Concern Opinions (GCOs), fostering further fine tuning actions of regulatory frameworks across the world.

## 2.1 Looking for a Framework of Analysis: The Seminal Work of Carson et al. (2013)

Carson et al. (2012) published a very long working paper titled "Audit Reporting for Going Concern Uncertainty: A Research Synthesis" aimed at outlining the state of the art of the entire plethora of researches related to GCOs. The intent beyond that huge research was fostering the debate and providing the PCAOB with a strong background useful to move on in a fine tuning action of auditing standards related to GC. In fact, Carson et al. mainly reviewed studies coming from the USA (or based on USA data and auditing practices). As a result of Carson et al.'s great efforts, in 2013 a very popular research article, with the same title as the working paper, has been published in *Auditing: A Journal of Practice & Theory* edited by the American Accounting Association, one of the best journals on auditing matters worldwide.

To our knowledge, Carson et al.'s work represents a cornerstone for moving on with the aim of providing a global picture as regards Audit Reporting for GCU

S. Brunelli, *Audit Reporting for Going Concern Uncertainty*, SpringerBriefs in Accounting, https://doi.org/10.1007/978-3-319-73046-2_2

academic debate. Any kind of research project should be accompanied by a review of the existing literature, for which the researcher has to define the relevant territory. This is fundamental for specifying the questions that will be answered throughout the study. Traditionally, a literature review can be structured in different ways, among which it is possible to distinguish the narrative and the systematic ones.

Most times an academic debate is based on a systematic literature review (SLR) and only when the topics or fields under investigation are very wide is a more narrative approach recommended. Audit reporting for GCU falls into the latter situation. As a matter of fact, the number of studies all around the world on this topic seem uncountable. That is one of the reasons why Carson et al. have separated studies on GCOs into three main categories:

- Determinants of GCOs;
- Accuracy of GCOs issued or not issued, by auditors;
- Consequences of GCOs on clients and auditors.

Within each category they individuated a series of features that feed other sub-clusters of analysis regarding specific aspects. This is particularly true for the determinants of GCO. Theoretically, as we partially saw in Chap. 1, reason(s) behind a GCO can be an indefinite number. Hence, scholars are free to study and detect the reason(s) by using different research methods (theoretical, case studies, archival, experimental etc.). Thus, the GCO research field is an open source even if it is evident that some areas are overexplored and others underexplored.

Table 2.1 provides Carson et al.'s categories; Tables 2.2, 2.3 and 2.4 provide evidence of the main features for each category.

In this chapter, using the same categorization, I provide a narrative literature review on GCOs in the USA (both resuming and updating, up to 2017, Carson et al.'s dissemination work), Europe and the rest of the world separately. The distinction among geographical areas is not based on the scholars' nationality, rather, it is based on country data used for the analysis (for quantitative researches) and/or on countries in which the firms or studies the authors made reference to are used for developing studies (for qualitative researches).

As will be made clearer later, the number and typology of studies, categories, features and aspects investigated by scholars differ considerably among countries, even in the same geographical area. Indeed, the reviewed papers are a collection of

**Table 2.1** Carson et al. studies on GCOs' categorization

| Carson et al. GCOs' categorization | | | | | | | | |
|---|---|---|---|---|---|---|---|---|
| Categories | | | | | | | | |
| **Determinants** | | | **Accuracy** | | | **Consequences** | | |
| Features | | | Features | | | Features | | |
| ... | ... | ... | ... | ... | ... | ... | ... | ... |

*Source* Author elaboration

**Table 2.2** Determinants of GCO

| Determinants | | | |
|---|---|---|---|
| Features | | | |
| Client factors | Auditor factors | Auditor-client/relationship | Environmental factors |
| Specific aspects | | | |
| ... | ... | ... | ... |
| ... | ... | ... | ... |
| ... | ... | ... | ... |

*Source* Author elaboration

**Table 2.3** Accuracy of GCOs

| Accuracy | | |
|---|---|---|
| Features | | |
| bankruptcy without a prior GCO | Prior GCO without bankruptcy | Variation of GCO accuracy across auditors |
| Specific aspects | | |
| ... | ... | ... |
| ... | ... | ... |
| ... | ... | ... |

*Source* Author elaboration

**Table 2.4** Consequences of GCOs

| Consequences | | |
|---|---|---|
| Features | | |
| For current shareholders | For future shareholders | For capital providers |
| Specific aspects | | |
| ... | ... | ... |
| ... | ... | ... |
| ... | ... | ... |

*Source* Author elaboration

a totally unbalanced panel used to draw out the essence of academic positions and future trends with regard to GCO. Even though the literature review has no systematic basis, many of the most popular academic research databases were used (Business Source Complete, Scopus, Web of Science, EconLit, JStor and Google Scholar) as well as other basic and sophisticated techniques of research, such as keywords usage (using different combinations) and the snowball papers extraction.

## 2.2   Studies and Trends in the USA

The USA represents the starting point of the literature. Firstly because of the referred work of Carson et al. and secondly because the majority of existing studies are based in the USA. Adopting the same categorization as Carson et al., studies regarding determinants, accuracy and consequences of GCOs are reviewed.

### 2.2.1   Determinants of GCOs

There exists a vast archival research stock intended to identify the characteristics causing the auditors to issue a GCO to an audit client. Through the analysis of these papers, four broad features can be identified as the determinants of a GCO:

- client factors;
- auditor's factors;
- auditor-client relationship;
- environmental factors.

Regarding the narrative literature review of USA researches on audit for GCOs, it is worthwhile noting that I decided to summarise research papers prior to Carson et al.'s first study (2012) only when, in my view, the results achieved from those researches by scholars are still valid and useful for the debate and/or when those studies have been useful or necessary to publish studies from 2012 onward.

#### 2.2.1.1   Client Factors

The issuance of a GCO is one of the most difficult decisions to be taken by an auditor, since he or she is in the centre of a moral and ethical dilemma, i.e. exposing a financially distressed firm, through a GCO, to an escalating risk; or not informing stakeholders of the reality through a missed GCO.

Traditionally, the literature provides numerous kinds of client factors that can determine the issuance of a GCO for a company. Among them, we may principally distinguish those factors (aspects) that are publicly available on financial statements, such as:

- profitability;
- leverage;
- liquidity;
- company size;
- debt defaults;
- prior GCOs.

And other factors which are not financial statements-related, such as:

- market variables;
- strategic initiatives;
- corporate governance characteristics.

In Carson et al. (2013), another three aspects were explored: financial reporting quality, corporate governance and book values and liquidation values. Notwithstanding the great efforts of the authors in classifying research articles into a useful cluster for analysis, I notice that the three mentioned aspects are quite residual, encompassing a very small number of research papers. However, in the last five years any relevant research articles related to these aspects have been produced. For this reason I will not provide any updates in this regard.

There are ten pivotal American works regarding client factors (Mutchler 1985; LaSalle and Anandarajan 1996; Behn et al. 2001; Davis 2010; Bruynseels and Willekens 2012; Vermeer et al. 2013; Feng and Li 2014; Mayew et al. 2015; Chen et al. 2016a, b, 2017a, b).

According to Mutchler, it is fundamental to consider confidential business information for issuing a GCO in the most accurate way possible. Responding to the attempt of the Auditing Standards Board (ASB) to eliminate the subject-to opinion[1] of 1982–1983, she asserted the importance of the access to inside information to produce an opinion able to reflect more than what can be gleaned from publicly disclosed information. Her research was based on the relationship between GCOs and the information available to the public. Mutchler performed a discriminant analysis to test GCO models with a sample of manufacturing companies that received a GCO and a sample of manufacturing companies that did not, even if they exhibited potential difficulties.

LaSalle and Anandarajan (1996) dealt with the possibility reserved for auditors on the issuance of either an unqualified audit opinion with modified wording or a disclaimer of opinion for entities with substantial doubt concerning GC. They identified through the use of logistic regression those factors that can push the auditors into choosing one of these two options. The results obtained indicated that having more bad news, less good news and a weaker internal control system, influenced the auditors more to produce a disclaimer of opinion. Furthermore, they evidenced the tendency to issue this kind of opinion for larger and publicly traded firms, especially for cases in which the auditors perceived the risk of being sued for the legal liabilities that would probably arise from their opinions.

From Management Discussion and Analysis (MD&A), auditors are able to apprehend management plans for the future of their firms. This information constitutes an important insight when considering the possible mitigating effects on the substantial doubt of the ability of the firm to continue as a GC. In their research, Behn et al. (2001) extended Mutchler's study. They modelled and tested the relationship between GCOs and three different types of management plan

---

[1]A prior way, used up to the 1990s, to express a GCO.

disclosures. After the realization of his empirical research, he concluded that GCOs are clearly connected to public mitigating information relating to management plans: in fact, plans to issue equity and to borrow additional funds appeared to be strongly associated with unqualified opinions. In 2015 Mayew et al. decided to continue the exploration of the effects of MD&A disclosure on the issuance of a GCO, as Behn et al. did in 2001. They undertook an analysis of a sample of firms that filed for bankruptcy between 1995 and 2012, in order to identify the predictive power of an MD&A over a GCO, accompanied by the disclosures of financial ratios and market-based variables. They concluded by ascertaining that MD&A has an incremental power extending to three years prior to bankruptcy.

The study conducted by Davis (2010) focuses on financial ratios and their values as indicators of financial distress, especially for those firms that, after receiving a GCO in Year 1, received an unqualified opinion in Year 2. His analysis went through the examination of 52 companies responding to these characteristics through the use of the Altman Z-Score model.

Feng and Li (2014) investigated professional skepticism about management earnings forecasts when making GC decisions. From the use of publicly issued management earnings forecasts, they discovered that there exists a negative association among auditor's GCOs, subsequent bankruptcies and management earnings forecasts. They evidenced that auditors pay lower attention to this kind of prediction, according to their perception; this is based upon the assumption that usually management earnings are way too optimistic, especially in those situations, predicting inflated high earnings for the organization. In the conclusion of their study, they succeeded in confirming that auditors are reasonably skeptical about management earnings forecasts when making GC decisions.

In recent years the relationship between audit reporting and business strategy has also been enlightened by scholars. In particular, a few are empirical researches on turnaround initiatives and their relationship with auditing reports. Bruynseels and Willekens (2012) focused on the link between GC decisions for distressed firms and business risk information. Through a study on a sample of firms in the U.S. manufacturing sector, their research finds that strategic long-term initiatives and short-term cash flow initiatives are both needed to have a mitigating effect on GCO decisions. The results seem to show that these initiatives are both associated with a higher probability of receiving a GCO. In addition, the results show differences in the mitigating effect of turnaround initiatives. Similarly, Chen et al. (2017a, b), using a sample of U.S. financially distressed firms, found that firms that use innovative strategies are significantly more likely than defenders to receive a GCO. These results suggest that business strategy is indeed a significant determinant for auditors interested in GCOs.

Lastly, a key part of the U.S. market is taken up by non-profit organizations; this part of the market has not been studied as much as the profit sector and can be useful to discover more details on GCOs. In this regard, an interesting research has been recently provided by Vermeer et al. (2013). They developed a model that takes into consideration different financial and non-financial measures such as: current debt, cash flow, restricted funds, expenses, Big 4, size, previous GCOs. The model's results showed that firms will have a higher risk of receiving a GCO if they are not in a good financial position, if they have saved more on programme activities, if they have a higher level of internal audit findings and the smaller they are. The model also showed that there is no relationship between audit firm type and type of audit opinion. In fact, 27% of the non-profit firms that received a GCO then filed for bankruptcy within the next four years. This study is important because it covers a sector that has had little research and can be used as a guideline for non-profit firms, their auditors and for comparison between profit and non-profit firms.

Lastly, Chen et al. (2016a, b) tested if and in which manner GCOs mighy determine an increase in the loan spread. They found that, on average, firms were issued a GCO pay 107 more basis points more than the others.

Table 2.5 details the studies on client factors, highlighting the aims and main results of each one.

### 2.2.1.2   Auditor Factors

Among the characteristics owned by the firms subject to a GCO, auditor firms can present some aspects influencing the issuance of this kind of opinion. Carson et al. in 2013 identified among them:

- auditor's economic dependence on the client;
- auditor size;
- auditor's judgement;
- industry specialization;
- auditor's compensation arrangements;
- auditor's organizational forms;
- auditor's psychology.

The majority of the literature analyzed is focused on the fees received by auditors and the resulting presence or lack of economic independence on the client (Ho 1994; Callaghan et al. 2009; Li 2009; Kao et al. 2014; Krishnan and Changjiang 2015; Read 2015).

Traditional literature on this topic has suggested significant agreement among auditors' GC judgements. In contrast, Ho (1994) discovered the existence of a missing agreement between more and less experienced auditors, who were given the same information about the financial health of the same problem company. Through the development of specific models, she succeeded in finding out that auditors with more expertise tended to express more positive GC judgements.

Subramanyam et al. started in 2002 to focus on this topic, as well; they evidenced that there is not some actual kind of association between non-audit fees and impaired auditor independence, or either total fees or audit fees, and the issuance of a GCO. Additionally, they discovered that this relationship is dominated by some other variables influencing the independence of the auditors, such as loss of

**Table 2.5** Studies on client factors

| Author | Year | Aim | Results |
|--------|------|-----|---------|
| Mutchler | 1985 | Determine the extent to which auditors' GCO decisions could be predicted using publicly available information | Ratios and prior-year opinion variable have predictive accuracy |
| LaSalle and Anandarajan | 1996 | Identification of some factors associated with auditors' choice between the two types of GC reports | Firms receiving a disclaimer are more likely to have more bad news items, fewer good news items, and weaker internal controls than firms receiving an unqualified modified report |
| Behn et al. | 2001 | Association between management plans (as suggested by SAS No. 59) and GCOs | Auditors' GCO decision is strongly associated to publicly available mitigating information relating to several management plans |
| Davis | 2010 | Analysis of the financial profile of 50 companies who were received a GCO in year 2 and received a clean opinion in year 1 | The Z-score analysis combined with the current ratio and cash flow from operations/current liabilities calculations provided an auditor with additional quantitative tools in supporting a decision to lift the GCM |
| Bruynseels and Willekens | 2012 | Study on the association between business risk information GC decisions for distressed clients | Short-term and long term (even potential) cash flow are necessary for strategic turnaround initiatives to mitigate the impact on the auditor's GC decision |
| Vermeer et al. | 2013 | Investigation into GCOs in non-profit organizations | Non-profits are more likely to receive a GC modified opinion if they are smaller, are in worse financial condition, expend less on programme-related activities, and have more internal control-related audit findings |
| Feng and Li | 2014 | The use of auditors' professional skepticism about management earnings forecasts during the valuation of the company's GC | Management earnings forecasts are negatively associated with both auditors' GCOs and subsequent bankruptcy |
| Mayew et al. | 2015 | Textual investigation of the information content in the MD&A section of a firm regarding its ability to continue as GC | The concern reported in the MD&A and the linguistic tone used provide significant explanatory power in predicting the firm's GC situation |
| Chen et al. | 2016 | Test, in the period 1992-2009, whether GCOs are associated with a hgher interest spread when contracting debt | Overall, authors find confirmation of the main hypothesis: the presence of GCOs determines an increase of 107 basis points on loan spread |
| Chen et al. | 2017 | Study about whether a firm's business strategy influences auditor reporting | Among a sample of financially troubled firms, prospectors are significantly more likely than defenders to receive a GCO |

*Source* Author elaboration

reputation and litigation costs. They represent some bollards to gaining the expected benefits from compromising the auditor independence.

Later, Li (2009) discovered that the situation described in Subramanyam's study has been modified; fee dependence and the incidence of a GCO moved from being insignificant in 2001 to being positive in 2003. In fact, after the SOX Act, auditors became more conservative, being aware of the public pressure they were subject to. Kao et al.'s study (2014) reinforced the same thesis, asserting the importance of the effect of major events and government regulations on auditors' independence, especially relative to the short-run.

However, Callaghan et al. (2009) reached different conclusions asserting that:

> When examining the relationship between the propensity of auditors to render GCOs and non-audit fees (and other auditor fees) for a sample of bankrupt U.S. firms, they did not observe any association between GCOs and non-audit fees, audit fees, total fees, or the ratio of non-audit fees to total fees.

Subsequently, two scholars investigated the same matter. Read (2015) did not find any evidence on the relationship between audit and non-audit fees and the probability of the issuance of a GCO through the analysis of a sample of 203 bankrupt companies during 2002–2013. At the same moment, Krishnan and Changjiang (2015) investigated the relationship between managerial ability, audit fees and GCOs. They concluded that the notion that managerial ability is relevant to auditors' decisions is true.

As explained before, it is clear that literature on this subject is controversial, but generally, the most diffused opinions tend to be negative about the interdependence between audit fees and GCO issuance.

Regarding the audit firm size, two groups of scholars expressed their positions: O'Clock and Devine (1995) and Carcello et al. (2000).The study conducted by O'Clock and Devine was focused on the influences of framed information and firm dimension on the auditor's GC decision in issuing or not a GCO. The results indicated that actually differences exist across firms according to their size. Carcello et al. confirmed the same results in 2000, when they examined the relationship between partner compensation, plans and client size and auditors' propensity to issue GCOs to financially distressed clients. However, they discovered that auditors in small-pool firms tend be more influenced by client size than partners in large-pool firms while making certain GCO decisions. However, these studies are essentially quite old considering the great changes in the U.S. economy in the last 15 years. Thus, new attempts in detecting the size of auditors and audited firms are encouraged.

Another aspect of the auditor that has been addressed in two studies is the psychological dimension of the issuance of a GCO for the auditors, that can feel themselves trapped in a typical situation akin to game theory. In 1992 Asare examined how differences in audit judgements were manifested in audit actions. In 1997 Matsumura et al. realized a game-theoretic model in which a client could potentially avoid a GCO and its self-fulfilling prophecy effect by switching auditors.

While there is still conflicting evidence on whether GCOs have information content or whether GCOs are predictable, the evidence relating to the accuracy of the GCOs is more pervasive. Table 2.6 lists the studies on auditor factors, highlighting the aims and main results of each one.

### 2.2.1.3  Auditor-Client Relationship

The auditor-client relationship is one of most addressed themes in the GCOs determinants area; in fact, 12 papers are, to our knowledge, points of reference in reviewing USA trends on this topic (Mutchler 1986; Biggs et al. 1993; Krishnan and Stephens 1995; Louwers 1998; Rau and Moser 1999; Maers et al. 2003; Venuti 2004; Krishnan et al. 2007; Fargher and Jiang 2008; Robinson 2008; Chan 2009; Read and Yezegel 2016).

By the auditor-client relationship, we mean that relationship, dynamic in nature, that includes switching, opinion shopping, personal relationships, and the time lag in opinion. Special attention is devoted to the auditor-client tenure and the personal relationship between auditors and client.

In 1986, Mutchler started to write upon this subject and, after analyzing the decision patterns of the auditors, she concluded that there was no evidence of the influence of the client-auditor relationship on the decision to issue a unqualified opinion or a GCO. She suggested that most of the auditors operated in accordance with the "procedure" described by SAS No. 34 (1981, the first US audit reporting standard to discipline the GCO modification).

In 1993, Biggs et al. developed a computational model, called GCX, in order to analyze the auditor expertise within the domain of the GC judgement. They focused on three broad categories of knowledge, expressly: financial, event and procedural knowledge. Through the use of the GCX model, they succeeded in extracting three different contributions:

- the GC judgement involves knowledge of specific events related to particular clients and the ability to reason about those events;
- GCX proposes four reasoning processes operating on financial and event knowledge to perform the GC task: problem recognition, causal reasoning about problems, evaluative reasoning about plans to mitigate problems, and a process that renders one of three GC judgements;
- a central component of the GC judgement is causal reasoning based on knowledge of actual client-related events, such as extensive knowledge of their client's operations, their client's industry, and world events that affected their client's financial problems.

In 1998, Louwers analyzed the relationship between auditor incentives and the decision to issue a GCO to a financially distressed firm. He conducted an analysis of 808 firms in trouble for the period from 1984–1991. He developed a model of the GCO decision as a function not only of the client's financial conditions and

**Table 2.6**  Studies on auditor factors

| Author | Year | Aim | Results |
|--------|------|-----|---------|
| Asare | 1992 | The impact given by several processing of evidence (considering also mitigating factors) on auditor's judgements | Auditors who evaluate information followed by mitigating factors issued more unqualified (fewer modified) opinions than those who evaluated the same evidence in the reverse order |
| Ho | 1994 | Auditors' GC judgements change taking into consideration the difference in the level of experience of the auditor | There is a lack of consensus among both experienced and less experienced auditors who were given information for a problem firm |
| O'Clock and Devine | 1995 | Effects of framed information and firm size on the auditor's GC report modification decision | Auditors are susceptible to the effect of framed information; this result changes across firm size |
| Matsumura et al. | 1997 | Investigation into the strategic interaction between auditor and client when the auditor is considering whether to convey an intention to issue a GC report | Client will never replace the incumbent auditor in a scenario in which the auditor is considering whether to convey an intention to issue a GC report |
| Carcello et al. | 2000 | Go in depth on the Association of partner compensation plans and client size with auditors' attitude to issue GCOs | No evidence that auditors' GCO decisions are directly affected by partner compensation plans; on the other hand, there is an interaction effect between partner compensation plans and client size |
| DeFond et al. | 2002 | Relationship between non-audit services fees and auditor independence | No significant association between NAS fees and impaired auditor independence |
| Li | 2009 | Relationship between client importance (proportion of audit fees, non-audit service fees, or total fees) and auditor independence (as propensity to issue a GCO) | Higher audit fee and total fee ratios are positively associated with the auditor's decision to issue a GCO. Post-SOX important clients have higher likelihood to receive GCOs |
| Callaghan. et al. | 2009 | Relationship between the propensity of auditors to render GC opinions and non-audit fees | There is no association between GC opinions and non-audit fees, audit fees, total fees, or the ratio of non-audit fees to total fees |
| Kao. et al. | 2014 | The association between fee dependence and the incidence of GCOs | Rise in auditor conservatism |
| Read | 2015 | Association between the propensity of auditors to issue GC opinions and NAS fees (and audit fees) | No significant relationship between GC decisions and NAS fees and audit fees |
| Krishnan and Changjiang | 2015 | Relationship between measure of managerial ability, audit fees and a GCO | Incremental to firm-level attributes, both audit fees and the likelihood of issuing a GCO are decreasing in relation to managerial ability |

*Source* Author elaboration

prospects, but also of factors associated with the auditor's loss function, which depends principally on prospective audit fees, auditor tenure and the client relationship.

In 1999, the study conducted by Rau and Moser evidenced the existence of possible biases in the decision to issue a GCO for those auditors with a certain amount of experience. These problems usually arise in situations in which there were some pre-existing relationships. At the end of their analysis, they concluded that:

> When provided with an identical set of information, seniors who performed another audit task for which the underlying facts of the case reflected positively (negatively) on the company's viability, subsequently made going-concern judgments that were relatively more positive (negative).

The "Weiss Report" (2002) was a study conducted with the purpose of providing information to the U.S. Senate on the incidence of bankruptcy in companies. This report constituted evidence for the deliberations of the SOX Act. In 2003, after the promulgation of the Act, Maers et al. reread the same report evidencing the point of criticism and the limitations of the information provided, especially in consideration of the auditor-client relationship and the accuracy of bankruptcy predictions.

In 2004, Venuti managed to address the same topic focusing on those firms that failed during the U.S. recession, which started in 2001.

Subsequently, the focus moved to the relationship between the auditor and client during the 2007–2008 crisis and its consequences. In 2007, a study was released by Krishnan et al. They examined GC modified audit opinions for former clients of Arthur Andersen, and compared them with opinions issued for other, newly acquired clients stating that:

> We find that auditors were less likely to issue going-concern modified audit opinions to small clients who switched from Andersen than to their existing clients. However, this trend reverses with an increase in client size, with large former Andersen clients more likely to receive going-concern opinions. Our results are consistent with suggestions that increased litigation risk associated with the larger ex-Andersen clients led to increased conservatism by the new auditors. We conjecture that the reduced conservatism for the smaller ex-Andersen clients is likely due to high ex ante conservatism of the Big 4 in not accepting clients perceived to be risky.

Going deeper through the consequences of the collapses of very important firms in the period from 2000 to 2002, Fargher and Jiang (2008) proved that auditors applied an increased conservatism in issuing their opinions and deciding on GCOs, reducing the incidence of failing companies without a prior GCO. Robinson in 2008 continued to investigate this relationship; in particular he examined whether the provision of a tax service could affect auditors' independence on the GCO decision, as it was recently prohibited by the Act mentioned before. This latter study was able to evidence how the provision of a tax service improved the likelihood of the issuance of a GCO prior to the company's failure, disproving the theories underlying the promulgation of the recent law.

In 2009, Chan investigated client importance and auditor independence within the local offices of audit firms. Distinguishing the period before the SOX Act (2001) and after (2003), he concluded that for the first case there was no evidence of this correlation, while the same could not be affirmed for the period after, especially for more important clients.

Other scholars tried to study more in depth the association between GCOs and auditor switching in case of GCO issue. The model used by Krishnan and Stephens (1995) found a positive relationship between the issue of the GCO and the possibility of a change in auditor. They also noticed that it is more probable that firms who change their auditors have already received that opinion before or will receive it after the switch to another auditor. These results show that firms do not obtain efficient results from a change in auditors or "opinion shopping" since both before and after the dismissal of an auditor they probably receive the same negative judgement. The problem of these results is that a switch of auditor does not necessarily mean that the firm is trying to "shop" its opinion and it could be caused by other factors. Even by removing, the more probable switches unrelated to "shopping" from the model's, results does not change but it is important to understand which are the alternative reasons for a switch to grasp all the topic and logic behind it. If instead the reason for this auditor change is caused by "shopping" of an opinion the results show unsuccessful effects of this "shopping". In addition, these results could be the effects of the additional standards imposed to avoid this practice used by firms, or the demonstration that the market autonomously avoids this situation without the need for new standards. All of these factors need further analysis to show an effective comprehension of auditor shopping.

Recently, in 2016, Read and Yezegel explored the possible association between auditor tenure length and audit failure (Type II error, that basically belongs to the accuracy feature, too) through the analysis of the audit reports for a sample of 401 U.S. publicly held companies that went bankrupt from 2002 to 2008. Their results indicated that long auditor tenure is not a factor of influence, but the overall evidence showed that audit failures were associated more often with the opinions produced by non-Big 4 auditors.

In conclusion, what emerges from the different analyses that were conducted is that there are some factors in the auditor-client relationship influencing the issuance of a GCO, especially for those periods that were not historically under the regulators' pressure. Table 2.7 lists the studies on auditor-client relationships, highlighting the aims and main results of each one.

### 2.2.1.4  Environmental Factors

Those factors that are external to the roles of the client, the auditor and their relationship can be addressed as environmental factors. The most important ones seem to be:

- the litigation environment;
- the auditing standards;
- audit procedure;
- audit wording.

On these topics, six papers decisively enrich the literature (Nogler 1995; Geiger and Raghunandan 2002; Chen et al. 2013; Kaplan and Williams 2013; Ference 2015; Daugherty et al. 2016).

The first insight that we can gather from this information is that the literature about this subject is relatively contemporary, with the exception of Nogler's study. This is a clear signal of the fact that the focus of the literature on GCOs moved only recently from looking for internal to external factors of influence. As the literature looks at all the concerns raised about the influence of the organization of the auditing standards, and also the audit wording and procedure, we can reconstruct a path in the evolution of the literature.

Nogler in 1995 provided a descriptive model of the procedure carried out by the auditors in order to issue a GCO on a client's financial statements. The conditions under which the opinions were and are currently issued were examined in relation to their resolutions, such as liquidation, dissolution, bankruptcy filing, or successful continuation of the firm. Successful resolutions were further analyzed to identify the characteristics associated with such successful resolutions. He concluded that the main sources of the factors influencing the issuance of a GCO can actually be traced to financial distress, but also to probability of litigation.

Twenty years later, Ference, after describing all the standards regulating disclosure on GC uncertainties, went deeper in analyzing the responsibilities of auditors; here are some data:

In an attempt to mitigate losses associated with a business failure, a client's lenders, shareholders, and bankruptcy trustees may pursue a claim against a CPA firm. Indeed, approximately 30% of claims brought against CPAs in the AICPA Professional Liability Insurance Program are made by third parties. Moreover, nearly 60% of the program's 2013 financial statement services claims related to the failure to detect a misstatement or a disclosure error, especially going-concern disclosures. These claims are found in all types of financial statement services, even reviews and compilations.

In AR Section 80—*Compilation of Financial Statements*, paragraph 20, it is stated that it is possible to omit the disclosures only if it is not misleading, but it is hard to believe that some lack of disclosure is not misleading. After that, Ference reported some of the most frequent GC claims, together with risk management tips. Then, she reported on the latest standards for accounting in 2014, expressly SSARS No. 21, *Statement on Standards for Accounting and Review Services: Clarification and Recodification* and Accounting Standards Update (ASU) No. 2014–15, *Presentation of Financial Statements—Going Concern (Subtopic 205–40): Disclosure of Uncertainties About an Entity's Ability to Continue as a Going Concern*, which was analyzed in Chap. 1.

In 2016, Daugherty et al. examined whether the differences in the wording of the GC standards in the U.S. affect auditors' decisions and the extent of the audit tests.

**Table 2.7**  Studies on auditor-client relationship

| Author | Year | Aim | Results |
|--------|------|-----|---------|
| Mutchler | 1986 | Factors (related to the guidance given by SAS No. 34) that influence the issuance of a GCO in a set of problem companies | Auditors follow the guidance offered by SAS No. 34 |
| Biggs et al. | 1993 | Introduce a new computational model of auditor expertise | The GCX model is reach in domain knowledge about the GC process, it considers auditors' behaviour and helps to understand what events may have led to a GC situation |
| Krishnan and Stephens. | 1995 | Investigation into audit opinion decisions for clients who switched, comparing the audit opinion decisions of the predecessor and successor auditors for clients who switched, relative to auditors' treatment of non-switching clients | No evidence were found |
| Louwers | 1998 | Investigation into determinants of GCOs related to the auditor's loss function | Auditors do not paid attention to factors such as litigations or negative operating results of client. Rather, they consider other indicators sympthomatic of a financial distress in fostering or not the issuance of GCOs |
| Rau and Moser | 1999 | Personal implication in other audit tasks and supervising seniors' GC judgements | Non Audit Services (tasks) have a greater influence on the senior's subsequent GC judgement |
| Maers et al. | 2003 | Investigation into the methodology adopted in the Weiss Report | The criteria adopted in the report had several incorrections leading to wrong forecasts for future bankruptcy |
| Venuti | 2004 | Investigation into the variables which cause the failure of auditors to issue a GCO during the U.S. recession | There are such assumption to accrual accounting that cause the failure in the issue of a GCO |
| Krishnan et al. | 2007 | Examination of how, overtime, Arther Andersen changes its opinion basing on the clients size | Auditors were less likely to issue GCOs to small clients who switched from Andersen than to their existing clients |
| Robinson | 2008 | The provision of tax services and its impact on auditor independence focusing on GCOs in bankrupted firms | Significant positive correlation between the level of tax services fees and the likelihood of correctly issuing a GCO prior to the bankruptcy filing |
| Fargher and Jiang | 2008 | Auditors' propensity to issue GC opinions before and after 2000-2002 (crisis period) | Auditors were more in favor to issue GCOs to financially stressed companies immediately after the US financial crisis |

(continued)

**Table 2.7** (continued)

| Author | Year | Aim | Results |
|--------|------|-----|---------|
| Chan | 2009 | Relationship between client importance (proportion of audit fees, non-audit service fees, or total fees) and auditor independence (as a propensity to issue a GCO) | Higher audit fee are positively associated with the auditor's propensity to issue a GCO. Post-SOX important clients have a higher likelihood to receive GCOs |
| Read and Yezegel. | 2016 | Association between auditor tenure length and audit failure (Type I and Type II misclassifications) | No significant association between auditor tenure and Type II errors for Big 4 audit firms; significant association analysing non-Big 4 firms |

*Source* Author elaboration

They conducted an experiment on the issue, discussing the fact that in the situation in which auditors were given the same data for a GC assessment, they produced different results, following distinguishable criteria for evaluation. In conclusion, the results they reported revealed that differences in wording can significantly affect auditors' conclusions.

Furthermore, we can analyze the risk of litigation in the GCO context, through the help of Geiger's, Kaplan's and Chen's contributions.

In 1995 the U.S. House of Representatives promulgated the Private Securities Litigation Reform Act which reduced the threat of litigation faced by auditors, especially in the case of a GCO issuance decision. The same concept was later asserted by SEC in 2000, evidencing the influence on auditors' behaviour.

Geiger and Raghunandan in 2002 examined the impact of that legal environment, through the analysis of the audit reports on 1,871 companies, which found themselves in financial distress during the period 1992–1993, 1996–1997, and 1999–2000. They outlined that the increase in the threat of litigation pushed the auditors to issue fewer and fewer GCOs, caused by the fear of committing a prediction error, that could probably cause a "self-fulfilling prophecy" effect.

The same topic represented the interest of the study conducted in 2013 by Kaplan and Williams. In particular, they investigated whether issuing a GCO to financially distressed clients can prevent auditors from being sued in a litigation. This litigation risk represents an endogenous factor influencing the supposed to be free auditor's decision. They came up with the following conclusions, obtained by the use of a simultaneous equations approach:

- there exists a negative association between going concern reporting and auditor litigation, suggesting that auditors deter lawsuits by issuing going concern reports to their financially stressed clients;

- when auditors are named in lawsuits, having issued a going concern report reduces the likelihood of large financial settlements.

Chen et al. in 2013 moved the focus of their research to insider selling and the risk of litigation: they first investigated the influence of insider selling on the issuance of a GCO and the subsequent consequences on the market; then, they focused their attention on the probability of attracting regulators' scrutiny and investor class action lawsuits, considering the previously mentioned factors. This concatenation of events can constitute an incentive to managers in pushing auditors for clean audit opinions. Through the use of empirical research, they concluded that actually the probability of receiving a GCO is negatively associated with the level of insider selling. In addition, they discovered that this negative relation is more pronounced for firms that are economically significant to their auditors, but the same cannot be affirmed when auditors have concerns about litigation exposure and reputation loss, and audit committees are more independent. Incidentally, this negative relation between GCOs and insider sales is significantly altered after SOX but in a less evident way. Table 2.8 provides studies on environmental factors, highlighting the aims and main results of each one.

## 2.2.2  Accuracy of GCOs

It is common to find studies examining the incidence of bankruptcy for firms without a prior GCO, or the proportion of firms who received a GCO, but do not subsequently fail.

These concerns made experts conceive two types of reporting misclassifications:

- Type I misclassification, arising when the auditor issues a GCO to a client, which does not subsequently fail;
- Type II misclassification, arising when the auditor decides not to issue a GCO to a client, which subsequently fails.

All the concerns on this topic are based on a statistical decision rule. Encountering both types of misclassification can result in potential costs:

- In the occurrence of a Type I misclassification, the auditor can bear the consequential costs of being dismissed as the auditor, for having caused the client to be perceived as unwdarranted and subsequently disgruntled,

    (a) For instance, $C\alpha$ represents the cost of lost audit revenues for the public accountant;

- In the occurrence of a Type II misclassification, the auditor may bear the costs related to litigation with the investors and the loss of reputation,

    (b) For instance, $C\beta$ is the cost related to the aforementioned consequences.

The auditor can decide to issue a GCO based on the possible economic incentives arising from the consideration of the ratio of the two costs, $C\beta/C\alpha$. In the situation in which the ratio is higher, the auditor prefers to issue a GCO since the cost of failing of doing is consistent (Matsumura et al. 1997; Carson et al. 2013).

**Table 2.8** Studies on environmental factors

| Author | Year | Aim | Results |
| --- | --- | --- | --- |
| Nogler | 1995 | Investigation into the influence given by corporate governance mechanisms on the propensity of directors to report fairly financial distress information | Information given by directors is often arbitrary and unhelpful to users, but robustness of corporate governance structures constrain directors to be more truthful in their GC disclosures |
| Geiger and Raghunandan | 2002 | The impact of the 'new' legal environment described after the SOX promulgation | GCOs were less likely (1) in 1996-97 than in 1992-93, and (2) in 1999-2000 than in 1996-97 |
| Kaplan and Williams | 2013 | Auditors' protection from litigation in the case of a issuance of a GCO to financially stressed firms | Significant positive association between auditors' ex ante litigation risk and GC reporting |
| Chen et al. | 2013 | The impact of insider selling on the likelihood of firms receiving auditor GCOs | The probability of receiving a GCO is negatively associated with the level of insider selling. This negative relationship is more pronounced for firms that are economically significant to their auditors but less pronounced when (1) auditors have concerns about litigation exposure and reputation loss and (2) audit committees are more independent. This negative relationship is significantly weakened after SOX |
| Ference | 2015 | Discussion on the professional liability of the American Certified Public Accountants (CPA) | When the accountant is aware of a GC matter, he/she is obliged to extensively address the issue |
| Daugherty et al. | 2016 | The differences in the wording of the GC standards in the U.S. affect auditors' decisions and the extent of the audit tests | The results reportedly revealed that differences in wording can significantly affect auditors' conclusions |

*Source* Author elaboration

The results extrapolated from the literature clearly indicate that the incidence of the "*proportion of firms filing for bankruptcy without a GCO is high, and the number of firms entering bankruptcy without a prior GCO in the population of audits is very low, often representing less than 1% of audit engagements.*" However, even a small percentage can cause dramatic consequences, such as economic loss to investors.

On this matter, the joint reading of 10 papers feeds the debate (Mutchler and Williams 1990; Hopwood et al. 1994; Tucker et al. 2003; Wertheim and Fowler

2005; Geiger and Rama 2006; Ryu and Roh 2007; Myers et al. 2014; Geiger et al. 2014; Yeh et al. 2014; Blay et al. 2016).

Mutchler and Williams in 1990 created the basis of this literature, investigating the relationship between audit judgement and the related type of technology used by the different accounting firms. They observed a higher degree of accuracy in the decisions of the auditors using a more structured approach. They also evidenced that there is a relationship between audit technology and the risk profile of the audit client base. In contrast, at the end of the study, a negative correlation was found between decision accuracy and audit structure.

Starting from the Cohen Commission (1978) and previous research, suggesting that GCOs are inferior indicators of bankruptcy in comparison to statistical models, Hopwood et al. conducted a study in 1994 that succeeded in confuting that statement. The empirical results they obtained provided evidence supporting the contrary of the notion previously stated. Nonetheless, neither the auditors' opinions nor the bankruptcy prediction model are foolproof predictors of bankruptcy.

Going directly to the research of the new millennium, we can examine the study produced by Tucker et al. in 2003. They conducted:

> ...an experimental economic test of a game-theoretic model of GCO judgment. Competing behavioral predictions are based on loss avoidance, risk seeking, altruism, and adversarial play...forecast accuracy, also has a significant effect on subject behavior: inaccurate forecasts did not lead auditors to express more clean opinions but led clients to switch auditors more frequently.

In 2005 Wertheim and Fowler focused on the accuracy of the GCOs, on the wave of the recent big failures of important firms, whose financial statements were audited by a giant, such as Arthur Andersen's public accounting firm. Their study presented an analysis of differences among audit firms in their propensity to issue a GCO for clients that subsequently filed for bankruptcy. It was conducted on a sample of 696 companies, which filed for bankruptcy between 1997 and 2001. The results produced indicated the existence of variations among Big-Five audit firm and non-Big-Five firms.

Continuing on the track marked by Wertheim, Geiger et al. (2014) analyzed the association between audit firm size and reporting accuracy, which historically provided mixed results. Their study, in particular, examined the amount of both types of reporting errors committed by the Big 4 audit firms over 11 years. Their results confirmed that Big 4 firms maintain constantly a higher reporting quality on GCOs than non-Big 4 firms.

Rye and Roh confirmed the same results in 2007 after having used a binary logit regression to analyze 1,332 firms that were non-bankrupt but financially stressed between 1997 and 1999.

On the wave of corporate accounting failures and regulatory proceedings, resulting in the enactment of the 2002 SOX Act, and the increased scrutiny of auditors, Myers et al. in 2014 investigated the change in auditor behavior with respect to GC reporting. On the one hand, they noted that non-Big N auditors became more conservative, decreasing their Type II misclassifications while increasing their Type I misclassifications. On the other hand, Big N auditors became more accurate, decreasing their Type I misclassifications with no corresponding increase in Type II misclassifications. In conclusion, the increased amount of auditor scrutiny operated by PCAOB succeeded in improving overall accuracy.

A more experimental approach was adopted by Yeh et al. in 2014: they conducted a study with the objective of increasing the accuracy of GC prediction through the use of a hybrid random forest (RF) and rough set theory (RST) approach, adopting Intellectual Capital (IC) as a predictive variable. They showed that this hybrid approach can represent the best classification rate with the lowest occurrence of Types I and II errors.

Geiger et al. continued their studies in 2014 concentrating on the consequences of the Global Financial Crisis. They examined auditors' GCO opinions for financially stressed clients that subsequently entered into bankruptcy during the period from 2004 to 2010. They discovered that both Big 4 firms and non-Big 4 firms increased their propensity to issue GCOs to subsequently bankrupted firms, resulting in a higher accuracy, contrasting the diffused belief of negligent auditors' behaviour during the crisis.

Recently, Blay et al. (2016) evidenced how increased doubt made the propensity to issue a GCO grow, due to economic and psychological factors. This higher propensity caused a higher incidence of auditors' Type I error rates without decreasing their Type II error rates. Their study questioned the diffused belief that a higher propensity of GCOs issuance always reflects higher audit quality.

Table 2.9 reviews studies on accuracy of GCOs, highlighting the aims and main results of each one.

## 2.2.3   Consequences of GCOs

The issuance of a GCO is likely to cause ulterior problems to already financially distressed firms. Prior to the GCO issuance, the concerns about substantial doubt represented private information, known uniquely by company's management and auditors. This information, moving from being private to public, is able to make reactions arise for two different categories of stakeholders of listed companies, such as:

- consequences for Shareholders;
- consequences for Lenders.

On the consequences of GCOs, I was able to distinguish 20 papers from the international academic debate.

**Table 2.9** Studies on accuracy of GCOs

| Author | Year | Aim | Results |
|---|---|---|---|
| Mutchler and Williams | 1990 | The audit structure (different types of technology) have an impact on auditor judgement | There is a negative correlation between decision accuracy and audit structure |
| Hopwood et al. | 1994 | Comparison between auditors' opinions and statistical models as predictors of bankruptcy | Auditors' opinions are not inferior to the statistical models in predicting bankruptcy |
| Tucker et al. | 2003 | Experimental economic test of a game-theoretic model on the impact given by the issuance of a GCO | Potential self-fulfilling prophecy reduces the number of GCOs and increases the likelihood of the client switching from the auditor. Accuracy also has a relevant impact on GCOs |
| Wertheim and Fowler | 2005 | Differences among audit firms in their propensity to issue a GCO for clients that subsequently filed for Chapter 11 bankruptcy | Interesting variations among Big-Five audit firms, as well as differences between Big-Five and non-big-five firms |
| Geiger and Rama | 2006 | Level of accuracy in Big 4 audit firms and in non-Big 4 companies | Both type I and type II error rates for Big 4 audit firms are significantly lower compared to non-Big 4 firms |
| Ryu and Roh | 2007 | Investigation into the materiality judgements and the auditor's propensity to issue a GCO to financially troubled but non-bankrupt companies | Big Six auditors (Five) were less likely to issue a GCO to their clients than non-Big Six auditors (Five) firms |
| Myers et al. | 2014 | The impact of the enactment of Sarbanes-Oxley Act (2002) on auditors' behaviour | Non-Big (six-five-four) were more conservative (issuing more GCOs) while Big (six-five-four) auditors were more accurate reducing type I and II errors |
| Yeh et al. | 2014 | Increase the accuracy of GC prediction by using a hybrid random forest (RF) and rough set theory (RST) approach | They proposed a hybrid approach has the best way to classify clients and the lowest occurrence of Types II and I errors |
| Geiger et al. | 2014 | Study whether auditors' GCO decisions were less likely after the start of the recent "Global Financial Crisis" (GFC) | The propensity of auditors to issue a GCO prior to bankruptcy significantly increased after the onset of the GFC |
| Blay et al. | 2016 | The rate of GCOs across different countries | Non-Big 4 auditors located in states with relatively high first-time GC rates in the prior year are up to 6% more likely to issue first-time GCOs |

*Source* Author elaboration

### 2.2.3.1  Consequences for Shareholders

With regard to the consequences of the GCO issuance for shareholders, I analyzed 15 studies which represent the thread of the entire issue (Fleak and Wilson 1994; Chen and Church 1996; Jones 1996; Carlson et al. 1998; Holder-Webb and Wilkin 2000; Blay and Geiger 2001; Elliot et al. 2006; Schaub 2006; Ogneva and Subramanyam 2007; Davis 2009; Menon and Williams 2010; Blay et al. 2011; Amin et al. 2014; Kausar et al. 2017; Khan et al. 2017).

The content of the GCO constitutes an incremental information for present and future investors. In an efficient market the returns on a firm's stocks are influenced by the expectations of the agents regarding the company's performance. Only new or unexpected information conveyed by the audit report would affect aggregate security prices.

The study conducted by Fleak and Wilson in 1994 provides evidence that the market distinguishes ex ante between firms that are deteriorating in financial condition and those that are not. Their market expectations approach used cumulative market-adjusted security returns to predict for the market's trend in each firm's expected cash flows. They concluded that unexpected auditors' GC qualifications are associated with abnormal security returns.

In 1996, Chen and Church deepened the research on the association between GCOs and the market's reaction to bankruptcy filings. They hypothesized that GCOs may reduce the surprise associated with bankruptcy: in fact, those companies that receive a GCO experience a less negative effect on returns in the period nearby bankruptcy than those receiving unqualified opinions, outlining the information value of the GCO.

In the same year, Jones assessed the information content of the GC evaluation made by auditors through the examination of the abnormal stock returns surrounding the publication of audit reports. He analyzed a sample of 86 audit reports with a GCO and a sample of 86 unqualified audit reports for financially distressed firms. He concluded, through the use of a portfolio test:

> that the mean abnormal return surrounding the release of the auditor's report was negative for firms which received going concern opinions and positive for distressed firms which received clean opinions. Ordinary least squares (OLS) regression tests indicated that mean abnormal returns surrounding the release of the auditor's report were lower for going concern opinions than for clean opinions and that the magnitude of the abnormal returns depended on the extent to which the opinion type was unexpected.

Carlson et al. (1998) studied the effect of a GCO on market valuation and they developed a covariance model (ANCOVA) which compared two sets of 88 firms, the first group with a GCO, and the control group without it. They found that financial statement readers find a going concern audit report (GCAR) useful for firm valuation purposes, contrary to prior research that found it confusing.

Holder-Webb and Wilkin in 2000 discovered that price responses to bankruptcy announcements were less severe for firms receiving GCOs than for firms receiving clean opinions

In 2001, Blay and Geiger tried to assess market reaction to GC report recipients. The results gathered through a multiple regression model indicated that a naive measure of market expectations was able to inform the market in an incremental measure to previously developed measures when using market reaction as an indication of changed expectations.

About the real estate market, in 2006, Elliot et al. were able to focus on the intra-industry information transfers from GCOs and the possible domino effect on competitive stock price reactions for other real estate firms. They found only moderate evidence

In the same year, Schaub conducted a broader research examining investor overreaction to the auditors' announcements of GCO issuances. He focused his analysis on evidence coming from 79 companies, receiving a GCO in the period 1984–1996. On the one hand, he was able to outline that the sell-off by investors on the announcement date was regularly followed by a major buy-back of the announcing firms' shares over the subsequent few days. On the other, the majority of the average losses on the announcement date, almost 70%, were regained in the following five days.

Two scholars, Ogneva and Subramanyam, conducted a comparative study on the differences of 12-months' market returns to first-time GCOs for Australia and USA in 2007. While the Australian market reacted in a modest negative way to the GCO announcements, the evidence from America suggested that the negative abnormal returns were associated with the choice of different expected returns.

Davis, in 2009, went deeper in analyzing the role of the GCO inside the financial market's system. Aware of the existence of the possibility of creating a self-fulfilling prophecy, increasing the cost and risk of extending credit to the beleaguered company, he analyzed the utility of this audit requirement. He examined the financial profile of 50 companies with a GCO in year 2 and that received an unqualified opinion in year 1, through the application of the Altman Z-Score model to the financial amounts and financial ratios.

In 2010, Menon and Williams managed to find evidence supporting the hypothesis of negative excess returns when a GCO was disclosed. This result was reinforced when the opinion expressly contained concerns about credit access, and the lack of respect of debt covenants, leading to even more negative returns. This effect was clearly coming from the reactions of institutional investors, since no detectable reaction at low levels of institutional ownership was found.

Blay et al. decided to continue their research in 2011, examining the proposition:

the auditor's going-concern modified opinion is a valuable risk communication to the equity market that results in a shift of the market's perception of financially distressed firms.

In conclusion, they were able to assess that results the market interprets the GC modified audit opinion as an important communication of risk, shifting the structure of the market valuation for firms, evidencing some degree of financial distress.

More recently, in 2014, Amin et al. focused on the relationship between the GCO and the cost of equity capital. They used two different samples, one for distressed firms and the other matched on propensity score. They documented a significant positive association between GCOs and rises in cost of equity capital.

In 2017, Kausar et al. deepened the research on the market's reactions with a brand new consideration focus: how legal regimes may affect the market's reaction to the auditor's GCO. They distinguished among two culture types: one is a creditor-friendly bankruptcy regime, such as the UK; the other is a debtor-friendly bankruptcy regime, such as the US. They observed that the first culture type reacted more adversely to a first-time GC opinion, indicating increased risk of loss associated with bankruptcy than investors do in the second culture type.

Lastly, in 2017, Khan et al. studied the effects of media news about GCOs on small and large trades. While the former are affected by the media, the second are not significantly influenced.

Table 2.10 resumes studies on consequences of GCOs for shareholders, highlighting the aims and main results of each one.


### 2.2.3.2  Consequences for Lenders

Regarding the consequences of the GCO issuance for lenders, seven studies decisively enrich the literature (Chen and Church 1992; Seipel and Tunnell 1995; LaSalle and Anandarajan 1997; Altman 1998; Foster et al. 1998; Feldmann and Read 2013; Amin and Harris 2017).

Chen and Church investigated the usefulness of default on debt obligations as an indicator of the issuance of a GCO. They analyzed a sample of 127 firms receiving a first-time GCO from 1982 to 1986 and a corresponding control sample, including firms possessing at least one problem company and receiving a clean opinion. Among them 98 were in default or in the process of restructuring their debt obligations to avoid subsequent default, while only one in the control sample found itself in default. They managed to show that auditors carefully consider default status in deciding whether to issue a GCO.

On the same track, Seipel and Tunnell 1995 went further in analyzing the contribution of GCOs to the decisions made by financial statement users. They focused on the association of such opinions with changes in risk, using different selection criteria for control firms, a different event window, and measuring risk shifts using Scholes-Williams beta.

In 1997, LaSalle and Anandarajan examined the difference in the reactions of bank loan officers to financial statements in the issuances of a disclaimer of opinion, rather than an unqualified report with an explanatory paragraph. They used between-subjects experiments to investigate loan officers' reactions to litigation occurrence:

> Results for litigation uncertainties show that a disclaimer (1) reduces the loan officers' willingness to grant a line of credit, (2) decreases loan officers' assessment of the entity's ability to service their debt, (3) reduces the assessed likelihood that the entity can improve its profitability, and (4) increases the point spread that would be charged if the entity was granted a loan.

**Table 2.10**  Studies on consequences of GCOs for shareholders

| Author | Year | Aim | Results |
|--------|------|-----|---------|
| Fleak and Wilson | 1994 | Aggregate security prices are subjected differently by expected or unexpected GCOs | The market distinguishes ex ante between firms that are deteriorating in financial condition and those that are not |
| Chen. and Church | 1996 | The association between GCOs and the market's reaction to bankruptcy filings | Firms receiving GCOs had less negative stock returns in the period surrounding bankruptcy concerns than those receiving clean opinions |
| Jones | 1996 | Stock market reactions to GCOs and stock market reaction to unqualified opinions received by financially distressed firms | Indipendently from the real degree of financial distress, firms received a GCO had higher negative abnormal returns then firms which did not receive a GCO |
| Carlson et al. | 1998 | Financial statement information (unexpected earnings, market returns, size, five financial ratios) are affected by GCARs | Users of inancial statement find a abnormal returns deriving form a GCO useful for firm valuation purposes |
| Holder-Webb. and Wilkin | 2000 | Verify if the expansion of requirements of SAS No. 59 impact on the price responses to bankruptcy announcement | Market price reaction is less negative for firms receiving SAS No. 59 |
| Blay and Geiger | 2001 | The use of a naive model to test markets' reaction to unanticipated modifications or anticipated modification, give a better result than previous models | There is the need for an improved model of market expectations |
| Elliott et al. | 2006 | The impact given by GCOs announcements on the stock market price of the competing companies | Modest evidence of the impact among rival firms |
| Schaub | 2006 | Investor overreaction to GCOs made in the major financial press | The sell-off by investors on the announcement date is followed by a major buy-back of the announcing firms' shares over the next few days |
| Ogneva and Subramanyam | 2007 | Understand whether a modified GCO could influence the stock-market in the medium-term, following the auditors' report | They did not find any evidence that the GCO issuance is associated with abnormal negative market returns for the Australian sample |
| Davis | 2009 | Analysis on the financial profile of 50 firms who received GCOs in year 2 and received a clean opinion in year 1 | The Altman Z-SCORE is a reliable predictor of a GCO |

(continued)

**Table 2.10** (continued)

| Author | Year | Aim | Results |
|---|---|---|---|
| Menon and Williams | 2010 | Investigation into the value relevance of GCO | Negative excess returns when the GCAR is disclosed |
| Blay A. D. et al. | 2011 | Market's perception of a financially distressed firm changes in presence of GCO | When a company receives a GCO the market evaluation has focused more on its balance sheet than on both balance sheet and income statement |
| Amin et al. | 2014 | Link between the going concern opinion and the cost of equity capital | GCOs foster an increase of the cost of equity capital |
| Kausar et al. | 2017 | The impact given by different legal regime on the market's reaction to GCOs | Investors in a creditor-friendly bankruptcy countries react more negatively to a first-time GCO, than debtor-friendly bankruptcy countries |
| Khan et al. | 2017 | Investigation on whether the press release on GC modification has effects on small and large trades | Small trades observe abnormal release at the event date at around. No significant effects were detected for large trades |

*Source* Author elaboration

In 1998, Foster et al. undertook a study to empirically investigate the relationships between loan defaults, violation of loan covenants, GCOs, and bankruptcy in bankruptcy prediction models, as Chen and Church had done in 1992. Foster et al. focused on two objectives:

- empirically testing the ability of loan defaults/accommodations and loan covenant violations to assess the failure risk;
- investigating the impact of failure to control for the aforementioned distress events on results from tests of the usefulness of GCOs in assessing bankruptcy risk.

They concluded that loan default/accommodation and loan covenant violation can both represent significant explanatory variables of bankruptcy prior to the event.

Altman in 1998, on the course plotted by Chen and Church and Foster et al., found evidence of the incidence of concurrent, or near concurrent, default-bankruptcy. He observed that default-bankruptcies were less common in the 1980s than the 1990s. Additionally, he observed that in half of the cases examined, the bond default date was identical to the bankruptcy date.

Much more recently, in 2013, Feldmann and Read explored the concerns about credit ratings information and GCOs for companies facing imminent bankruptcy. They applied logistic regression to financially distressed companies that filed for bankruptcy from January 1, 2000 to June 30, 2009 and were able to show that:

...the likelihood of an auditor issuing a GC opinion is associated with the credit rating issued by Standard & Poor's (S&P) preceding the audit report date. In results supporting the idea that the auditor's opinion has informational value, the paper also finds that after issuance of a GC report, S&P's credit rating tends to be downgraded.

Lastly, in 2015, a unique study was proposed by Amin and Harris. They tested the consequences of GCOs in non profit organizations on three types of stakeholders: donor, service recipients and managers. Overall they found that a GCO has positive and negative effects depending on stakeholder and organization type.

Table 2.11 resumes studies on the consequences of GCOs for lenders, highlighting the aims and main results of each one.

**Table 2.11**  Studies on consequences of GCOs for lenders

| Author | Year | Aim | Results |
|---|---|---|---|
| Chen and Church | 1992 | Verify the usefulness of default status in explaining the weak association between the issuance of GCOs and the occurrence of bankruptcies in auditing | Auditors consider default status in making GC decisions. They rigorous applied the procedure stated in SAS No. 59 |
| Seipel. and Tunnell | 1995 | Analysis of the association of such opinions and changes in risk | The increase of a unsystematic risk is associated with the issue of a GC qualified opinion |
| LaSalle. and Anandarajan. | 1997 | The different reaction of bank loan officers to financial statements accompanied by a disclaimer of opinion rather than an unqualified report with an explanatory paragraph | Disclaimer of opinion (1) reduces the possibility for granting loans, (2) decreases loan officers' assessment of the entity's ability to service their debt, (3) reduces the assessed likelihood that the entity can improve its profitability |
| Foster et al. | 1998 | Investigation of relationships between loan defaults, violation of loan covenants, GCOs, and bankruptcy in bankruptcy prediction models | "Loan default/accommodation and loan covenant violation are both significant explanatory variables of bankruptcy" |
| Altman | 1998 | The utilization of debt defaults and GCOs in bankruptcy risk assessment | The incidence of concurrent, or near concurrent, default-bankruptcy dates were less common from the 1980s well into the 1990s |
| Feldmann and Read | 2013 | Relationship between credit ratings and GCOs | Credit rating have influence on GCO decision making process |
| Amin and Harris | 2015 | Test the consequences of GCOs for non profit organization on three class of stakeholders: managers, service recipients and donors | GCOs are value relevant, having positive and negative effects depending on stakeholder and organization type |

*Source* Author elaboration

## 2.3  Studies and Trends in Europe

Analyzing the academic debate in Europe related to Audit Reporting for GCU presents a higher complexity. There are three main reasons:

- the lack of a research synthesis, such as that performed by Carson et al. for the USA. Thus, the framework needs to be contextualized for Europe;
- the presence of a smaller number of studies in comparison with those for the USA;
- there are some differences in terms of perspectives and critical issues addressed in European studies. Hence, the same categorization adopted by Carson et al. is not always suitable for reviewing purposes.

However, in order to allow the reader to use the same framework of analysis, I decided to adopt the same categorization. In addition, the debate, in the European context, differs for other structural reasons such as:

- different market size and structure;
- differences among sectors;
- differences in financial reporting standards;
- differences in the contextualization of the agency problem;
- smaller firm dimension, on average;
- partially different corporate governance systems and mechanisms.

Given these differences, the following paragraphs address the European academic debate on Audit Reporting for GCU in Europe.

### 2.3.1  Determinants of GCO

Similarly to the American side, four broad features can be identified as the determinants of a GCO:

- client factors;
- auditor factors;
- auditor-client relationship;
- environmental factors.

#### 2.3.1.1  Client Factors

Information found in financial statements can lead auditors to issue GCOs depending on the idea they have of the company's global health. This idea can be applied to the financial information of the company, evaluating different factors of the company, such as profitability, liquidity, leverage, size and if it has had debt defaults. There are different studies that find associations between the issuance of a GCO and different financial and non-financial measures of the companies.

As previously mentioned, another three residual aspects were explored: financial reporting quality, corporate governance and book values and liquidation values. Differently from the US side, some studies related to these features will be discussed for Europe because of their relevance for the academic debate.

Above all, there are seven studies that seem most relevant for the debate (Laitinen and Laitinen 1998; Ireland 2003; Ruiz-Barbadillo et al. 2004; Arnedo et al. 2008; Tsipouridou and Spathis 2013; Gallizo and Saladrigues 2016; Wu et al. 2016).

Laitinen and Laitinen (1998), in their model, found a relationship between a higher probability of receiving a GCO and poor profitability, high leverage or debt and a low level of growth. The model used by these authors uses 16 financial measures: net profit, operating cash flow, net sales, total assets, percentage change in net sales, ROE, ROI, equity to debt, quick ratio, debt to net sales, net sales per employee, operating cash flow per net sales, net profit per net sales, a bankruptcy risk measure, number of employees, and the average payment period for accounts payable. Their research found that the chance of being qualified as in distress for big Finnish firms will be higher as the growth of the firm decreases, as the part of the firm that is financed by equity decreases and as the number of employees decreases.

Ireland's (2003) work covers several determinants that can have an effect on GC and audit reporting in the UK. With his model, Ireland finds results that indicate high levels of liquidity and constant payments of dividends as two positive signals that lower the possibility of receiving GCOs, while having a high level of liabilities, having losses and with high debt to equity are factors that could increase the probability of receiving a GCO. Another minor factor that had an effect on the possibility of a GCO was the size of the firm: the smaller the firm the higher the possibility of a GCO. Ireland's analysis helps research on determinants by indicating with a multivariate analysis that a firm that had already received GCOs in prior periods had more probability of receiving GCOs again. However, the model also indicated that subsidiary firms that hired larger auditors, had less possibility of receiving GCOs. The research then proceeded to analyse if the type of company, listed or non-listed, had any effect on GCOs' results by analysis of both public and private companies. In the first univariate results, listed companies had a significantly lower probability of receiving a GCO modification than non-listed companies. Nevertheless, these results were not confirmed in the multivariate test, since no evidence was found that listed or public companies had a different effect on reporting modifications. The only difference that was confirmed in both tests was that subsidiary companies were more likely to receive GCOs than independent companies.

In recent years there have also been interesting studies about the relationship between GCOs and financial reporting quality. Tsipouridou and Spathis (2013) show no significant relevance of discretionary accruals and GCOs; this means that auditors do not take into account this information when reporting. Thus, it seems that a low financial reporting quality is not detrimental in fostering a GCO issuance.

The authors agree by saying that the variability in the GC decision is better explained by financial characteristics such as poor financial performance in the current fiscal year, prior year losses, audit opinion type received in the previous year and small firm size. In fact, as a result of Greece's crisis, an increasing number of GCOs were issued between 2010 and 2011.

With respect to recent times, studies indicate profitability, indebtedness and the company's liquidity as key factors in the advance detection of the inclusion of GCOs. Based on these factors Gallizo and Saladrigues (2016) focused on five selected variables in the Spanish financial environment:

- Return on Assets (ROA), which signals that the more positive the economic profitability ratio, the lower the probability of the company receiving a GCO;
- Short-term Debt, because it is one of the biggest threats for Spanish companies; the higher the ratio, the higher the probability that a firm will receive a GCO;
- Current Ratio, as one of the most important ratios and because it has been inserted in most of the studies about financial data used to predict GCO. There are conflicting results but most of the time a positive high ratio has an inverse relationship with the possibility of receiving a GCO;
- Liquidity Ratio, as a measure of the ability of a firm to comply with its financial obligations; the greater the level of liquidity coverage a company has, the lower the possibility of receiving a GCO;
- Size, expressed as the volume of the company's assets. Usually the bigger a company is, the lower probability it has to receive a GCO (the well known claim "too big to fail");
- Lastly, they add a binary variable expressing whether the company had a loss (1) or not (0).

Their model finds that firms that had less net losses and lower levels of financial distress will have a lower chance of receiving a GCO. One of the most important factors underlined in their study was not the relationship of a GCO with present losses but with long-term recurring losses, highlighting how harmful they are in leading to a GCO. Gallizo and Saladrigues found that in the 48 companies analysed in 2012, a greater level of current ratio, ROA and company liquidity, would decrease the possibility of a GCO.

Regarding the effects on financial reporting quality on the audit opinion, Ruiz-Barbadillo et al. (2004) searched for connections between a distressed company receiving a GCO and audit quality. The process of the decision making of auditors is considered in this research and has been divided into different stages. Firstly, the model looks for a possible GC distress, then it analyses if it is capable of causing the company enough critical distress to induce the auditor to issue a GCO. The model takes its sample from 1199 non-financial Spanish firms between 1991 and 2000. The results indicate that audit quality does indeed have an effect on the probability that a firm in financial difficulty would receive a GCO. This association is valid not only for the auditor's capacity to find financial uncertainties, but also for the decision of auditors regarding the kind of opinion to issue.

Arnedo et al. (2008) deepen the knowledge of audit related to the GC assumption, through two events that have not been analysed particularly in research on audit: the earnings overstatement and the wording used by auditors in the GC qualifications. They found many differences between discretionary accruals of Spanish GC and non-GC companies. Moreover they found that large parts of GC uncertainties are not written clearly and with a high amount of conditional language by the auditor. The results of the research outline the necessity to improve the mechanism of implementation, as GC audit standards are not adequate by themselves to efficiently control auditor behaviour. The research has not found signs that indicate the reason for wording differences is caused by the company's financial condition or other auditor motives. Even if Big 4 auditors do issue a greater number of GCOs, it is also probable that they are using wording strategy in the years in proximity to the failure. The analysis has provided proof that the Big 4 use of differentiation of words does indeed happen but tends to decrease as the companies reach bankruptcy. The results found in Arnedo et al.'s paper fortify the need to increase the implementation process that increases quality of auditors, since high quality audit standards have not been sufficient.

Finally, interesting evidence of the relationship between a GCO issuance and corporate governance mechanisms and settings has been provided by Wu et al. (2016). These authors search for a relationship between audit committee characteristics and the possibility of receiving GCOs by UK bankrupt firms. Their study starts by analysing the danger presented by auditor NAS (national audit services) to auditor GC decisions but it does not find any important link between NAS and the probability of receiving a GCO. However, it shows that the NAS and auditor GCO issuance relationship depends mostly on the attributes of the audit committee. In this case, it finds that clients with lower numbers of independent non-executive directors (NEDs) and financial specialists have less probabilities of being provided a GCO before failing. These results contribute to provide corporate governance regulators with an explanation of the relationships between audit committee independence and the level of financial specialization, and the auditors conclusion on GC. Table 2.12 lists studies on client factors, highlighting the aims and main results of each one.

### 2.3.1.2 Auditor Factors

Among others, the auditor factors that are more enlightened on the European side are the auditor's economic dependence on the client and the auditor size (Firth 2002; Basioudis et al. 2008; Hope and Langli 2010; Quick and Warming-Rasmussen 2015).

The impact on auditors that fees, incentives and the possibility of being dismissed have on their GCOs is an important issue. These effects could lower the efficiency of the GC reports and put at risk more investors.

At the beginning of the 21$^{st}$ century, Vanstraelen (2003) stated that an auditor, in choosing whether or not to disclose GCU in the audit report, potentially faces

**Table 2.12** Studies on client factors

| Author | Year | Aim | Results |
|---|---|---|---|
| Laitinen and Laitinen | 1998 | Develop a logistic model based on financial statement information to identify qualified audit reports | A reliable model to explain GC qualifications in the audit reports of Finnish environment with respect to publicly-traded companies |
| Ireland | 2003 | Multinomial logit model to analyse the determinants of both GC and non-GC related audit modifications (for listed and non-listed companies), including modifications for disagreements and limitations on scope | The determinants of audit reports differ between different types of audit opinions modification. In addition, subsidiary companies hiring big five are significantly less likely to receive clean opinions, whereas, non-subsidiary companies appointing large auditors are significantly more likely to receive GCOs |
| Ruiz-Barbadillo et al. | 2004 | Investigates the relationship between audit quality and the probability that a financially distressed company would receive a GCO | A GCO is a function on both the company's financial troubles and auditor independence. This means that the auditor's knowledge and experience have no effects on GC decisions |
| Arnedo et al. | 2008 | Significant differences between the discretionary accruals of Spanish GC and non-GC firms | Supports the need to strengthen the enforcement mechanisms that affect auditor incentives. The existence of excellent auditing standards is not enough in avoiding auditor abuses or to improve the quality of auditor reporting in roman codified countries |
| Tsipouridou and Spathis | 2013 | Relationship between audit opinions and earnings management, as measured by discretionary accruals, for listed firms on the Athens Stock Exchange (ASE) | Audit opinions are not related to earnings management. Client financial characteristics, such as profitability and size are determinants of the GCO decision |
| Gallizo and Saladrigues | 2016 | Relationship between GCAO and some features of the firm and auditor, including financial distress | The t probability of obtaining a GCO is more a function of persistent losses rather than a sudden decline of the firm's financial position |
| Wu et al. | 2016 | Associations between audit committee features and the likelihood of auditors' GC decisions | Failed firms with higher proportions of independent Non Executive Directors and financial experts on the audit committee are more likely to receive GCOs prior to bankruptcy, but there is no significant relationship between NAS fees and the likelihood of receiving a GCO |

*Source* Author elaboration

economic obstacles, in terms of the cost of loss of the client, being sued by a third-party and harm to reputation. She chose Belgium as the setting for her study, since nearly all the already published documents on GC had focused on the Anglo-American framework, which has a higher risk of litigation than among Belgian companies. Indeed, she discovered that in Belgium auditors were less likely to issue a GCO if they had been paid high audit fees and had incurred a loss of clients in the previous year.

To better isolate the effects of auditor factors, Vanstraelen also tested some client factors such as:

a. financial condition of the client;
b. location of the client;
c. delay in holding the annual general shareholders meeting; and
d. bad news regarding the Board of Directors.

Specifically, the results suggest that the GCO decision is significantly correlated to recent loss of client, and the higher the audit fees the less the propensity of the auditors to issue GCOs. No association was found between the auditor's GCO decision and the other factors mentioned above. An exception is, of course, the influence of bad news about the Board of Directors and the company in general: Vanstraelen showed that these have a significantly negative effect on GCO decisions from auditors.

Quick and Warming-Rasmussen (2015) analysed the different possibilities of causes that put at risk the independence of an auditor. These could be caused by individual services, which were studied to understand if there is statistical evidence of this effect and is so what that effect is. Their study analyses data from Germany and finds that high self-interest, any benefit that could be received by the auditor, high familiarity threats, excessive sympathy towards the company, could compromise the auditor's decision.

The problems of audit fees is also analysed in the UK to try to resolve the issue of the possible effect of fees on the reporting decision of the auditor. Only Geiger's previous study had found a relationship between high fees and lower possibility of an issuance of GCO caused by economic dependence. Firth in 2002 and Basioudis et al. (2008) in the UK setting find statistical evidence that GC issuance is related to NAS fees and auditor fees. Their robust results confirm the concern of regulators and investors that these fees can bias auditor opinions. Regulators can use this study to find a way to regulate NAS fees since they result more influencing.

In Norway, Hope and Langli tested if the loss of auditor independence could be higher among private client firms than for publicly trade in a low litigation environment such as Norway that reduces the expected costs to the auditor associated with independence impairment. The authors tested whether auditors who receive higher fees are less likely to issue GCOs. In spite of their boost hypotheses they did not find evidence Table 2.13 points out studies on auditor factors, highlighting the aims and main results of each one.

**Table 2.13**  Studies on auditor factors

| Author | Year | Aim | Results |
|---|---|---|---|
| Firth | 2002 | Relationships between NAS fees paid to auditors and audit fees, and the occurrence of qualified opinions | There is a positive association between consultancy fees and audit fees, and this is determined by some firm-specific events that generate a needs for consultancy services as well as additional audit efforts |
| Basioudis et al. | 2008 | Investigation about audit reports provided to companies in trouble waters in the UK and the magnitude of audit and NAS fees paid to the firm's auditors | The magnitude of both audit fees and non-audit fees are associated with the GCO release. As a matter of fact, stressed firms with high audit fees are more likely to receive a GCO, whereas companies with high non-audit fees are less likely to receive GCO |
| Hope and Langli | 2010 | Test for auditor independence impairment among (1) private client firms, in a low litigation environment (i.e., Norway) | The fee level's is not detrimental on the auditor independence |
| Quick and Warming-Rasmussen | 2015 | Investigation related to the effect of such features on independence perceptions in the case of German investors | A high self-interest and a high-familiarity features may impair auditor independence in appearance. In fact, a significant effect on investors' trust in auditor independence is not revealed |

*Source* Author elaboration

### 2.3.1.3  Auditor-Client Relationship

In Europe, in recent years, two aspects have been mainly investigated by scholars with regard to the auditor-client relationship: auditor switching, rotation and tenure; and opinion shopping (Lennox 2000; Vanstraelen 2003; Ruiz-Barbadillo et al. 2006; Knechel and Vanstraelen 2007; Ruiz Barbadillo et al. 2009; Vandenbogaerde et al. 2011; Barnes and Renart 2013; Garcia-Blandon and Argiles-Bosch 2017).

Vanstraelen (2003) analysed what would be the effect of a GCO on the firm or the effect it could have on the auditor. The research focuses on the possibility of auditors avoiding GCOs for fear of retributions in the form of loss of prestige or for fear of a change in auditor. Belgium's accounting standards require a company to keep an audit firm for a minimum of three years, which can be used as samples to show if there are different effects on the first, in which the auditor knows that it cannot be dismissed, and last years of this period. These standards could help measure the effects on auditors if the results of each year are compared, since the effect of auditor switching should be more believable from the last of the three years than from the first. The results of this research confirm this by showing a probability of four times lower in the first years than in the last year, if the company had received a GCO.

Vandenbogaerde et al.'s study uses a sample of private Belgian firms of 2006 to search for the possibility that there is a relationship between auditor independence and its dismissal and if this relationship is caused by the prestige of the firm. Although the analysis does not find significant data to confirm this hypothesis, it does find that clients have less probability of receiving GC modifications if their clients are in the last year of their contract. Nevertheless, the analyses find data that link high accruals have the probability to be welcomed by auditors that have a higher possibility of being sent away.

As regards the opinion shopping practice, many studies used models that compared GC results before and after the auditors' dismissal. Lennox decided to analyse the effect of audit shopping by evaluating the consequences that this would have had on firms if they made contradictory decisions with the auditor, both in firms that use this technique and firms that do not. The results show, as expected, that there is a higher probability for an auditor to be dismissed after submitting a GCO. In addition, the research also finds results of a lower probability of a GCO if the auditor changes.

More recently, Barnes and Renart (2013) investigated more in depth a specific feature of the relationship between auditor and client: the auditor's bargaining power. First, they explained that the auditor might be under pressure, leading to the kind of error where there is no prior GCO, but the company fails afterwards (Type I error). In this case, the results are clearly attributed to the lower bargaining power of the auditing firm. In contrast, they noticed that the auditors may succeed in resisting any pressure from the company not to issue GCOs when the auditing firm has less economic dependence, so that it has a relatively higher bargaining power with its clients. Obviously, this study is in line with the ones presented above, in particular Vanstraelen (2003) and Ruiz-Barbadillo et al. (2004), in which auditors' independence is measured against their willingness to issue or not GC qualifications. The aim of Barnes and Renart in their research is to explain that the independence of auditors is not subject to the needs of the client-company or the need of the auditing firm to "survive", but that shareholders and investors require a fair and clear evaluation of the firm. Building on these assumptions, the researchers chose Spain as a ground field to examine these issues, since the Spanish auditing environment is unregulated but highly concentrated. Moreover, since smaller Spanish companies are also being audited, its capital market is relatively denser, resulting in lower dependence by investors on audited financial statements. Barnes and Renart introduce their analysis starting from an assumption on the GC errors. These are classified into three categories: the first is caused by the lack of experience and understanding of the auditor of the sector where the client has its business (the "incompetence hypothesis"); the second is caused by auditors' economic concerns (the "lack of independence hypothesis")[2]; finally, despite auditor's ability and independence, the result is far away from what is estimated. Although there is the certainty that the entity will or will not fail, the chance of error can still occur. In the end, Barnes and Renart discovered a high tendency of Spanish auditors to give GCOs, independently from the pressure of clients. Moreover, the significant results on Type I error let us understand that Spanish auditors are willing to issue qualified opinions to protect their reputation ("over-conservatism"), meaning that companies in Spain have less influence on auditors' decisions. Finally, this research is coherent with what Ruiz-Barbadillo et al. (2009) suggested about the reputational issue brought to life after the revocation of mandatory auditors' rotation in 1994.

Despite discretion, the decision to include the GCO in the report cannot be deferred any longer in terms of risk. This happens when the auditor forces the company to adjust its balance sheets downwards.[3]

Ruiz-Barbadillo et al. (2006), in their research, plan to supply more evidence about opinion shopping and its effects on different aspects of the connection between auditors and firms. This research is needed because the evidence up to 2006 has not been enough to give efficient options to standard regulators to assure that the GCO will not be influenced and that it will not be putting investors at higher risk. By increasing the knowledge in these arguments, researchers are trying to discover if clients do indeed use types of pressure to change the opinions they could receive. In their study, a relationship is found between the period that the auditor has been in his position of judgement on that firm and the probability of decline in opinion shopping. This link between judgement and tenure could be caused by the auditor's intention to keep his/her contract with the firm until the latter has recovered part of their monetary profit. After this profit is achieved, auditors start to evaluate more the risk of losing their status and take decisions by evaluating other factors. These seem to be the explanations that explain more efficiently auditors' behaviour over time, showing that they are more dependent on the firms' pressure at first, while gradually becoming more independent in their decisions while occupying that presssure.

---

[2]Either the auditor resists disclosing a GCO to avoid the loss of clients, or the auditor is firmly convinced of the need to give a qualified opinion to protect his/her reputation.

[3]The auditor encourages revealing hidden liabilities and eliminating overpriced assets that may be overstated in the balance sheet to show a more solvent image.

Also Knechel and Vanstraelen (2007) analysed the association that could exist between audit quality and the period of time the auditor has been in his position. The research focuses on data from Belgian private companies in distress in which there is less possibility of disagreements between auditor and client. This setting is the perfect place to search for a possible association between tenure and audit quality but in this case does not show a decrease in quality of audit reports that have been made by auditors that have spent more time serving that client. The paper's results find no significant association of an effect of audit tenure on audit quality; this could be through different causes linked to the Belgian environment or because the sample they analyse includes only small, private, distressed firms. In the end even though these results do not find any association between the two, they do not conclude that there is no effect of auditing tenure in the EU countries and this encourages further investigation to find these results.

Garcia-Blandon and Argiles-Bosch (2017) are interested in analysing the relationship between audit quality and the period the auditor has worked for the client because of the EU regulations that have been implemented in 2014 to avoid loss of audit quality. To understand if standards of this new rotation policy are needed, the paper analyses a sample composed of listed Spanish companies in the period between 2005 and 2011. The analysis seem to find a small, or almost no, significant effect between audit or partner tenure and audit quality, which depends on the probability of issuing GCOs, as it is seen in studies that evaluate this effect in other countries. However, between the change of firm as auditors, and the change of partner in the same firm, it is found that partner change has a more significant and strong effect than a complete change in auditor company. Table 2.14 lists studies on the auditor-client relationship, highlighting the aims and main results of each one.

### 2.3.1.4   Environmental Factors

As far as the environmental factors are concerned, I noticed, essentially, two important studies: Martin 2000 and Carcello et al. 2009. Both studies were aimed at exploring how much the differences in accounting and auditing standards across countries determine the differences in audit reports.

Martin (2000) compares different regulations that have been used in different countries to enhance the efficiency and accuracy of accounting and auditing, but their differences could be leading to different determinants of GCOs between countries. In general, audit and accounting standards are similar for every country but their little differences and the effect that they may cause is what Martin's paper researches. The model, with its sample of 122 public firms that are in high distress, shows significant evidence that the GCO in the US is issued with more probability than a GCO in France or Germany. These results are of great importance because it might mean that even with similar accounting standards for each country a GCO received in Germany or France might have a diverse meaning. In US firms, it was found that there was a higher probability of firms to have received a GCO for debt related factors. While with French firms, the model indicates that it is less probable

**Table 2.14** Studies on auditor-client relationship

| Author | Year | Aim | Results |
|--------|------|-----|---------|
| Lennox | 2000 | Test for opinion shopping by predicting the opinions companies would have received had they made opposite switch decisions | The auditor switching plays a decisive positive role in obtaining the desired opinion |
| Vanstraelen | 2003 | Examine the relationship between auditor economic incentives and the propensity to issue GCOs | Supports the contention that the auditor's GCO decision in Belgium is significantly associated with factors surrogating the perceived consequences of disclosing a GCU |
| Ruiz-Barbadillo et al. | 2006 | Investigation into the effect of long-term audit contracts on the likelihood of a company's engaging in opinion shopping | There exists a relationship between the length of audit engagement and the probability of opinion shopping |
| Knechel and Vanstraelen | 2007 | An exam of effects of auditor tenure on audit quality for private firms | The auditor tenures does not affect the auditor indipendence. On average, the evidence for tenure either increasing or decreasing quality is not found or weak |
| Ruiz-Barbadillo et al. | 2009 | Investigation on a ten years time span (1991–2000) aimed at revealing if the mandatory or not mandatory rotation affects the audit reporting behaviour | They did not find evidence about significant difference in the audit reporting behaviours during the passage from not mandatory to mandatory rotation |
| Vandenbogaerde et al. | 2011 | Investigation on the likelyhood that a client dismisses the incumbent auditor has an impact on the auditor's impairment of independence and whether this association is conditional on the importance of the client in the audit partner's client portfolio | The likelihood of an auditor dismissal has no effect on the attitude of releasing a GCO for financially distressed firms |
| Barnes and Renart | 2013 | Test of Spanish auditors attitude in releasing qualified opinions to protect their reputation | Results point out a high attitude by auditors to issue GCOs undeterred by pressure from client firms |
| Garcia-Blandon and Argiles-Bosch | 2017 | Impact of firm and partner tenure on audit quality, where audit quality is proxied by discretionary accruals | Without considering the interaction effects, firm and partner tenure do not seem to play a relevant role as determinants of audit quality. Importantly, the interaction of firm and partner tenure shows stronger effects on audit quality than both forms of tenure separately considered |

*Source* Author elaboration

to have management changes or firms' takeovers then in US companies. Firms from Germany instead had more management changes then French firms but fewer takeovers than US firms. As a summary of his research, Martin noted that:

**Table 2.15** Studies on environmental factors

| Author | Year | Aim | Results |
|--------|------|-----|---------|
| Martin | 2000 | Comparison of accounting and auditing standards for GCU across three countries—France, Germany, and the U.S.—belonging to different accounting and auditing cultures | Country-specific standards were essentially similar across countries, but financial reports revealed significantly higher GCOs incidence for U.S. firms than other countries, even when controlling for firm-specific features that might be associated with GCOs |
| Carcello et al. | 2009 | An exam of the potential effects in shifting form principle based to rules based standards after 2000 | A relationship was found between the nature of GC audit standardsand auditor reporting on financially stressed companies |

*Source* Author elaboration

The observation of the difference in disclosure practices, though, is important to users because they must be aware that similar disclosures (or lack of disclosures) across countries may not have the same meaning. Failure to consider country-specific influences on GCU disclosure practices might lead investors to misestimate the level of uncertainty associated with the GC assumption when evaluating company risks and prospects.

Anyway, many steps ahead have been made since Martin's study. Notwithstanding, it remains a cornerstone that could drive scholars to address the issue of differences in standards.

Carcello et al. (2009) researched if the important new regulation imposed by the Belgian government in 2000 had the effect it intended to have on the quality of GCOs. Through a sample of Belgian private firms, the model analyses the effect of the change in regulations and the additions in the auditor's role to control for two new financial criteria, with which the firm must be aligned. Their research finds evidence on two important effects caused by the new regulation. Thanks to the new regulation if the firms are in accordance with the two new criteria, there is a lower probability that the auditor will issue GCOs when firms do not risk going bankrupt and there is a higher probability that the auditor will issue a GCO when firms are about to go bankrupt. This analysis shows that the intent of the regulations to give more responsibilities to auditors, so investors will feel more protected after the recent crises, is having the desired effect. Table 2.15 provides studies on environmental factors, highlighting the aims and main results of each one.

## 2.3.2   Accuracy of GCOs

As referred to when I expanded on the US academic debate, there might be two types of reporting misclassifications:

- Type I misclassification, arising when the auditor issues a GCO to a client, which does not subsequently fail;
- Type II misclassification, arising when the auditor decides not to issue a GCO to a client, which subsequently fails.

Sometimes, it occurs that Type II error can be caused not by auditors' inability, inexperience or conservatism. Another related factor has geographical and psychological roots: the proximity to areas affected by a high rate of GCOs. In Europe, excluding a few studies related to Belgium and the UK (Citron and Taffler 1992; Lennox 1999; Knechel and Vanstraelen 2007) there is a distinct lack of studies detecting in depth the accuracy rates of GCOs. Most of the times when and where these data are provided they represent the ground for studying other features and aspects or audit reporting for GCU.

For instance, studies have been conducted on the effects of the interaction between auditing standards and institutional factors, since their combined impact can affect auditor's decision-making. Prior researches demonstrated the significance of legal settings (e.g. those protecting more investors or with strong enforcement) in elucidating the differences across financial markets in several countries. Despite this attention paid to the interactions between accounting, finance and law, there is little research on how legal regimes influence investor response after the auditor issues a GCO. In particular, Kausar et al. (2017) have recently analysed how legal regimes (creditor vs. debtor-friendly code law) may influence investor response to the increased financial distress risk determined by the issuance of GCOs. They took US and UK bankruptcy law as the sample, and determined how the different aspects of the two may impact on market reaction. Specifically, finance and legal scholars observed that the US is built more towards the rights of the debtor, thus protecting a firm's GC status; whereas, UK safeguards more the rights of the creditor, thus liquidation processes are more likely. As a consequence, the authors believe that GCOs represent a negative signal to market investors more in the UK than in the US, in light of the different legal treatment of claimholders. Therefore, the results demonstrated that bankruptcy law will determine the informativeness of the GCO to capital market participants, as shown by the differential market reaction to GC announcements in both countries. This is in line with the belief that, in spite of the equality of this negative public signal, market investors will react more unpleasantly in a creditor-friendly than in a debtor-friendly bankruptcy system.

Table 2.16 outlines studies on the accuracy of GCOs, highlighting the aims and main results of each one.

### 2.3.3   Consequences of GCOs

As we have seen, the market reactions to audit opinions could have consequences not only for current and future shareholders, but also for lenders and other capital providers.

**Table 2.16** Studies on accuracy of GCOs

| Author | Year | Aim | Results |
|--------|------|-----|---------|
| Citron and Taffler | 1992 | Likelihood of firm failure, auditor switch rates, the self-fulfilling prophecy and audit firm size are studied as variables potentially affecting the value of the audit report when GCOs are released | The probability of receiving a GCO is strongly associated with a decline of economic conditions of the firms. There is some evidence in support of an association between the presence of a GCO and auditor switching but no other associations were found |
| Lennox | 1999 | Evaluation and explanation of the accuracy and informativeness of audit reports in identifying failing companies | (1) a bankruptcy model could be better than audit reports in predicting financial distress overtime (2) audit reports have not incremental information in signaling the probability of bankruptcy |
| Knechel and Vanstraelen | 2007 | An exam of effects of auditor tenure on audit quality for private firms | The auditor tenures does not affect the auditor indipendence. On average, the evidence for tenure either increasing or decreasing quality is not found or weak |
| Kausar et al. | 2017 | How a legal regime may affect the market's reaction to the auditor's GCO | Code and bankruptcy law and investor's reaction |

*Source* Author elaboration

Over time, also in Europe, some studies have addressed the issue of the so-called self-fulfilling prophecy phenomenon as the bankruptcy of a company that could have survived without receiving any GCO. In this respect scholars find validations (Gaeremynck and Willekens 2003; Vanstraelen 2003) and contradictions (Citron and Taffler 1992; 2001).

On the same subject, the literature which reveals a negative (or in a few cases, positive) stock reaction to different types of audit opinions, is extensive. Firth (1978), considering a sample of 247 observations in the UK market, found a small negative stock price reaction to GCOs. Several years later, Taffler et al. (2004), and Soltani (2000), confirmed the results achieved by Firth (1978). Soltani (2000) analysed the French market; he considered a larger sample (543 observations) and showed significant negative abnormal returns around the audit opinions releases. Pucheta-Martínez et al. (2004) analysed the Spanish market and found opposite results.

As regards Italy, only one study has been released in this specific research area. Ianniello and Galloppo, in 2015, showed that, on average, the qualifications expressed in the audit reports containing a GCO of the Italian listed companies had negative effects on the respective stock prices. At the same time, they highlighted

**Table 2.17** Studies on the consequences of GCO

| Author | Year | Aim | Results |
|---|---|---|---|
| Firth | 1978 | Measure of the abnormal returns associated with various "types" of qualification | Some types of audit qualification had a significant impact on investment decisions while others had very little. There was found to be no relationship between the accounting firm qualifying the accounts and the abnormal returns |
| Citron and Taffler | 1992 | Likelihood of firm failure, auditor switch rates, the self-fulfilling prophecy and audit firm size are studied as variables potentially affecting the value of the audit report when GCOs are released | The probability of receiving a GCO is strongly associated with a decline of economic conditions of the firms. There is some evidence in support of an association between the presence of a GCO and auditor switching but no other associations were found |
| Soltani | 2000 | Searching for evidence about the relationship between audit modifications and stock prices in France | Significant negative abnormal returns are revealed around audit opinions announcements |
| Citron and Taffler | 2001 | Investigation about possible auditor's decision to not issue a GCO to avoid subsequent bankruptcy of the audited firm | No evidence was found |
| Gaeremynck and Willekens | 2003 | Relationship between audit-report type and subsequent business stop for private companies in a low litigation environment | An endogenous relationship exists between bankruptcy and audit-report type, and between voluntary liquidation and audit-report type |
| Vanstraelen | 2003 | Examine the relationship between auditor economic incentives and the propensity to issue GCOs | Supports the contention that the auditor's GCO decision in Belgium is significantly associated with factors surrogating the perceived consequences of disclosing a GCU |
| Taffler et al. | 2004 | Stock price reaction to UK GCOs after the audit reports releases | The sample evidenced underperforms by between 24% and 31%, depending on the benchmark adopted |
| Pucheta-Martínez et al. | 2004 | Test whether there is a relationship between audit modifications and stock prices in Spain | Modified audit reports were not value relevant for investors |

(continued)

**Table 2.17** (continued)

| Author | Year | Aim | Results |
|---|---|---|---|
| Ianniello and Galloppo | 2015 | Examine investor reactions to auditor opinions containing qualifications or an 'emphasis of matter' paragraph related to GC uncertainty or financial distress | Audit reports investigated have information content for investment decisions. Qualifications expressed in the audit report have a negative effect on stock prices. An unqualified opinion with an emphasis of matter paragraph regarding GCU or financial distress has a positive effect on stock prices |

*Source* Author elaboration

that unqualified opinions containing a GCO positively affect stock prices. Using the Event Study methodology (ES), they analysed a data set covering 2007 to 2010, containing 97 observations from 41 unique firms.

Chapter 3 is dedicated to provide empirical evidence of Italian investors' perceptions of GCOs alongside the last global financial crisis (2008–2014). Thus, further insights about the relative literature are provided there. Table 2.17 resumes studies on the consequences of GCO, highlighting the aims and main results of each one.

## 2.4 Studies and Trends in the Rest of the World

In this Sect. 2.1 shall analyze and discuss the main studies regarding the GCO and its effects in other countries around the world.

In Australia, the two researches undertaken by Herbohn et al. (2007) and Ogneva and Subramanyam (2007) discovered that in the period following the disclosure of the GCO there is no evidence of any causal relation. Herbohn et al. (2007), further discovered that not only in the medium-term period following the disclosure of the report were some effects caused by the modified opinion present, but also in the short-time window. The only significant effect discovered by them was on the 12-months period prior to the disclosure of the auditors' report, which has shown a negative abnormal return on the stock market. These results are due to the fact that in Australia a continuous disclosure regime is present.

On the other hand, evidence from China provides a different outcome in comparison with the Australian one. In fact, the two studies conducted by Chen et al. (2000, 2017a, b) wanted to investigate, in the first one, the effect of modified audit opinion on the stock price, considering the GCO only as a dummy variable, whilst the more recent study had a focus on GCO as a real explanatory variable. What has emerged from Chen et al.'s researches is that in a short-term period around the disclosure of a modified audit report the market reacted negatively; nevertheless the most severe effect was recorded on the GC case which, in the days following the disclosure of the report, had an average effect of −4.23% on the stock price. Instead in the long-term, no significantly negative effects on the stock price have been found, rather a slightly positive effect, justified by the author as compensation for the higher risk faced by the investors. However, also in China there is literary evidence of a causal relationship among GC modified audit opinions and future firms' financial performance.

Another research study by Chen et al. (2016a, b) explored the possibility of a company using opinion shopping to influence the report that it receives. Proof and the effects of audit opinion shopping have only been found in insignificant or unreliable ways and standards regulators do not have enough evidence to implement any effective regulations. The model shows that, to be successful in opinion shopping, a firm has an association with the type of the audit firms' organizational forms and the level of importance of the company that is being audited. In addition, the model shows that the firms that use this scheme to influence auditors are associated with higher accounting accruals, and lower profits. It is also confirmed that auditors that are being sent away have a lower probability of not issuing a GCO in comparison to the new auditors that are replacing them. The research also takes into consideration the stepping down of auditors at their own discretion and their replacement with partners of the same audit company. An example of this could be a partner that is conservative and not inclined to risk that prefers to change his role with a partner that is more inclined; this could lower the probability of a company receiving a GCO.

China, but in the People's Republic, has been studied using the same hypothesis as in the Taiwanese market (Hsu et al. 2011). The authors found a negative market reaction around the preparation and disclosure of the auditors' report, also showing an information leakage towards investors. Unluckily for the purpose of their study, no causal relationship between GCO and stock price fluctuation has been found, instead the negative market reaction could be due to other factors. What has been found as a main discovery is a negative market reaction around the disclosure of the GC modified report, but effects change from country to country.

As has been discussed for the USA and Europe studies, the effects of a modified GC report are not limited only to oscillation in the market's prices or returns, but have also been linked to the self-fulfilling prophecy. Incidentally, it has been demonstrated in Australia (Carey et al. 2008), in China (Ting et al. 2008), in Japan (Shirata and Sakagami 2008) that this phenomenon does not exist. Default factors in these countries arise from other variables contained in the financial statements. The only country where a slightly positive correlation has been faced between the two phenomena was Canada (Cormier et al. 1995), but results may not be a fair representation as this paper was quite old and the method applied to reach the results was different from the ones used today. In fact, it has been successively demonstrated that even in Canada a relationship between the two does not exist, and even if, globally speaking, the GCO increases a little bit the probability of default, claiming the existence of a self-fulfilling prophecy, is quite far from reality.

Another phenomenon that has been detectedis auditors' reluctance to issue a first-time GCO as clients could shift, as it has been demonstrated that receiving a GCO is a statistically significant phenomenon that increases the probability of auditor switching; causing losses for the auditors and even for the firm that is changing the auditing company as they have to pay for a new service (Carey et al. 2008). In fact, to support the previously mentioned theory of Carey et al., and to further investigate the phenomenon, it has been shown that to avoid auditor-switching many local auditing firms have underreported the actual situation of a firm (Young and Wang 2010). It has also been demonstrated that the global financial crisis, over the whole market, has propelled GC reporting, as the number of reports containing this modification has significantly arisen thanks to the crisis. This increase of GC reporting has also been demonstrated to be present in Australia (Xu et al. 2013).

As with the global financial crisis, also local financial crises could replicate the phenomenon of the increase in reporting; the 1997 Asian Financial Crisis has been studied, to understand if those effects could be found even in a low-litigation risk environment. The conclusion reached by this study was a positive reply that highlighted the increase in reporting and the professionalism of Chinese auditing firms (Lam and Mensah 2006). This result has been steadily confuted, claiming that there was no scientific or statistical evidence that justified the results obtained in Hong Kong (LaSalle and Anandarajan 1996).

It has been further analyzed if other economic phenomena could influence the GC reporting quality, such as a change in policy (Mo et al. 2015), or regulatory sanctions (Firth et al. 2014). The results obtained from the first study, related to the 2006 Chinese Bankruptcy Law are not as relevant, in fact it has been shown that the issuance of this new law did not influence the major Chinese auditors; only the local top-10 ones showed an improvement in conservatism, whereas the smaller ones continued to report with the same low quality. As the second study has shown, regulatory sanctions, differently from changes in policy, have had a significantly positive effect on the increase in GC reporting and shaping auditors' behaviour, as auditors to face themselves in situation of sanctions, or to avoid legal consequences, became more conservative. As a matter of fact, this is a field still open for discussion, as results are often discordant. The general line is that a GCO affects the stock market, but it is not an unavoidable doom for a company receiving it. Future researches and papers will clarify the doubts and the discordancy remaining. Table 2.18 lists studies on GCOs in the rest of the world, highlighting the aims and main results of each one. It is worth to note that there are no relevant studies addressing the accuracy of GCOs in the rest of the world, Hence scholars are encouraged to fill this gap.

**Table 2.18** Studies on GCOs in the rest of the world

| Author | Year | Country | Determinants (D); Consequences (C) | Aim | Results |
|---|---|---|---|---|---|
| Cormier et al. | 1995 | Canada | D, C | Understand the variables and factors that cause a GCO issuance, and whether this kind of opinion could mean a bankruptcy determinant for companies receiving it | Financial and liquidity ratios have been found to be a cause for GC issuance. A positive correlation between GCO and failure has also been found |
| Chen et al. | 2000 | China | C | Understand whether there exists a relationship between GCO and future performance, and the successive effects during the short- and long-term | Evidence has been found of abnormal returns around the disclosure of the modified audit reports |
| Lam and Mensah | 2006 | China | C | Understand whether auditors reported accurately even in a low-litigation environment such as the Chinese one | They discovered that the analyses performed by Chinese auditors were as accurate as the US ones even if they were in a low-litigation environment |
| Herbohn et al. | 2007 | Australia | C | Understand whether a modified GCO could influence the stock market in the short- and medium-term | There is no statistical evidence of a change in price following the modified auditor report, but negative market effects have been registered in the 12-months period prior to the disclosure of the report |
| Ogneva and Subramanyam | 2007 | Australia | C | Understand whether a modified GCO could influence the stock market in the medium-term, following the auditors' report | They did not find any evidence that the GCO issuance is associated with abnormal negative market returns for the Australian sample |

(continued)

**Table 2.18**   (continued)

| Author | Year | Country | Determinants (D); Consequences (C) | Aim | Results |
|---|---|---|---|---|---|
| Carey et al. | 2008 | Australia | C | To understand the causal relationship among GCOs, and how it could affect the decision of switching an auditor compared to other kinds of reports. Second, whether there is an increase in probability for a company to fail after receiving a GCO | It has been shown that receiving a first-time GCO increases the probability of a company to switch auditing firm. No evidence has been found of any relationship between failure and issuance of a GCO |
| Shirata and Sakagami | 2008 | Japan | C | Understand whether the issuance of a GCO was the factor that doomed the bankrupted companies in the Japanese environment | They did not find any evidence that the GCO could mean the subsequent failure of a company, denying the possibility of a self-fulfilling prophecy |
| Ting et al. | 2008 | China | C | Understand whether the issuance of a GCO was the factor that doomed the bankrupted companies | They did not find any evidence that the GCO could mean the subsequent failure of a company, denying the possibility of a self-fulfilling prophecy |
| Hsu et al. | 2011 | Taiwan | C | Understand whether there exists a relationship between GCO during two events, the Audit Report filing and the Announcement day, and the market returns | Abnormal negative returns have been found five days after the audit report day |
| Xu et al. | 2013 | Australia | C | Understand if after the Global Financial Crisis auditors had more propensity to issue GCOs for risky clients | They discovered that the Global Financial Crisis positively influenced auditors' behaviour in issuing GCOs. A further discovery was that Big 4 firms anticipated the Global Financial Crisis, increasing the accuracy of GC reporting sooner than other firms |

(continued)

**Table 2.18** (continued)

| Author | Year | Country | Determinants (D); Consequences (C) | Aim | Results |
|--------|------|---------|-----------------------------------|-----|---------|
| Firth et al. | 2014 | China | C | Understand whether the issuance of a sanction against auditors could improve the quality of their reports | Sanctioned auditors have more propensity to issue a GCO |
| Mo et al. | 2015 | China | C | Understand whether the 2006 Chinese Bankruptcy Law has changed Auditors' behavior in misrepresenting the fair view of a company | The law improved only the top-10 local auditing firms, as the Chinese Big 4 were almost at a higher level, to defend their international image. No effects have been shown on the minor local auditors that continued with the previous behaviour |
| Chen et al. | 2016 | China | D | Study if companies engage partners shopping within the same audit company | Companies are used to engage in partner-level opinion shopping. This happen more when the audit firm is a partenership than a corporation |
| Chen et al. | 2017 | China | C | Understand whether there exists a relationship between GCO and future performance, and the successive effects during the short- and long-term | A relation has been found between GCO and future performance, but the effects are only noticed in the short-term, whilst in the long-term there is no statistically significant effect |

*Source* Author elaboration

# References

Altman EI (1998) Discussion: an analysis of the usefulness of debt defaults and going concern opinions in bankruptcy risk assessment. J Account Audit Finan 13(3):373–374

Amin K, Harris EE (2017) Nonprofit stakeholder response to going-concern audit opinions. J Account Audit Finan 32(3):329–349

Amin K, Krishnan J, Joon SY (2014) Going concern opinion and cost of equity. Audit A J Pract Theory 33(4):1–39

Arnedo L, Lizarraga F, Sanchez S (2008) Going-concern uncertainties in pre-bankrupt audit reports: new evidence regarding discretionary accruals and wording ambiguity. Int J Audit 12 (1):25–44. https://doi.org/10.1111/j.1099-1123.2008.00368.x

Asare SK (1992) The auditor's going-concern decision: interaction of task variables and the sequential processing of evidence. Account Rev 67(2):379–393

Barnes P, Renart MA (2013) Auditor independence and auditor bargaining power: some Spanish evidence concerning audit error in the going concern decision. Int J Account 17(3):265–287. https://doi.org/10.1111/ijau.12003

Basioudis IG, Papakonstantinou E, Geiger MA (2008) Audit fees, non-audit fees and auditor going-concern reporting decisions in the United Kingdom. Abacus 44(3):284–309

Behn K, Steven E, Krumwiede KR (2001) Further evidence on the auditor's going-concern report: the influence of management plans. Audit A J Pract Theory 20(1):13–28

Biggs SF, Selfridge M, Krupka GR (1993) A computational model of auditor knowledge and reasoning processes in the going-concern judgment. Audit A J Pract Theory 12(2):82

Blay AD, Geiger MA (2001) Market expectations for first-time going-concern recipients. J Account Audit Finan 16(3):209–226

Blay AD, Geiger MA, North DS (2011) The auditor's going-concern opinion as a communication of risk. Audit A J Pract Theory 30(2):77–102. https://doi.org/10.2308/ajpt-50002

Blay AD, Moon JR, Paterson JS (2016) There's no place like home: the influence of home-state going-concern reporting rates on going-concern opinion propensity and accuracy. Audit A J Pract Theory 35(2):23–51

Bruynseels L, Willekens M (2012) The effect of strategic and operating turnaround initiatives on audit reporting for distressed companies. Account Organ Soc 37(4):223–241. https://doi.org/10.1016/j.aos.2012.03.001

Callaghan J, Parkash M, Singhal R (2009) Going-concern audit opinions and the provision of nonaudit services: implications for auditor independence of bankrupt firms. Audit A J Pract Theory 28(1):153–169

Carcello JV, Hermanson DR, Huss HF (2000) Going-concern opinions: the effects of partner compensation plans and client size. Audit A J Pract Theory 19(1):67–77. https://doi.org/10.2308/aud.2000.19.1.67

Carcello JV, Vanstraelen A, Willenborg M (2009) Rules rather than discretion in audit standards: going-concern opinions in belgium. Account Rev 84(5):1395–1428

Carey PJ, Geiger MA, O'Connell BT (2008) Costs associated with going-concern-modified audit opinions: an analysis of the Australian audit market. Abacus 44(1):61–81. https://doi.org/10.1111/j.1467-6281.2007.00249.x

Carlson SJ, Glezen GW, Benefield ME (1998) An investigation of investor reaction to the information content of a going concern audit report while controlling for concurrent financial statement disclosures. Q J Bus Econ 37(3):25–39

Carson E, Fargher NL, Geiger MA, Lennox CS, Raghunandan K, Willekens M (2013) Audit reporting for going-concern uncertainty: a research synthesis. Audit A J Pract Theory 32 (1):353–384. https://doi.org/10.2139/ssrn.2000496

Chan L (2009) Does client importance affect auditor independence at the office level? Empirical evidence from going-concern opinions. Contemp Account Res 26(1):201–230

Chen C, Xiumin M, Xin W (2013) Insider trading, litigation concerns, and auditor going-concern opinions. Account Rev 88(2):365–393

Chen CJP, Su X, Zhao R (2000) An emerging market's reaction to initial modified audit opinions: evidence from the Shanghai Stock Exchange. Contemp Account Res 17(3):429–455. https://doi.org/10.1506/GCJP-5599-QUWB-G86D

Chen F, Peng S, Xue S, Yang Z, Ye F (2016a) Do audit clients successfully engage in opinion shopping? Partner-level evidence. J Account Res 54:79–112. https://doi.org/10.1111/1475-679X.12097

Chen KCW, Church BK (1992) Default on debt obligations and the issuance of going-concern opinions. Audit A J Pract Theory 11(2):30–49

Chen KCW, Church KB (1996) Going concern opinions and the market's reaction to bankruptcy filings. Account Rev 71(1):117–128

Chen PF, He S, Ma Z, Stice D (2016b) The information role of audit opinions in debt contracting. J Account Econ 61(1):121–144

Chen S, Hu B, Wu D, Zhao Z (2017a) When auditors say 'no', does the market listen. Working paper

Chen Y, Eshleman JD, Soileau JS (2017b) Business strategy and auditor reporting. Audit A J Pract Theory 36(2):63–86

Citron DB, Taffler RJ (1992) The audit report under going concern uncertainties: an empirical analysis. Account Bus Res 22(88):337–345

Citron DB, Taffler RJ (2001) Ethical behaviour in the U.K. audit profession: the case of the self-fulfilling prophecy under going-concern uncertainties. J Bus Ethics 29(4):353–363

Cormier D, Magnan M, Morard B (1995) The auditors' consideration of the going concern assumption: a diagnostic model. J Account Audit Finan 10(2):201–222. https://doi.org/10.1177/0148558X9501000201

Daugherty B, Callaway DC, Dickins D, Higgs J (2016) The terminology of going concern standards. CPA J 86(1):34–39

Davis RR (2009) Financial ratios influencing the issuance of auditor's going concern opinions. Proc Northeast Bus Econ Assoc:65–68

Davis RR (2010) Financial ratios influencing the lifting of auditor's going concern opinions. Proc Northeast Bus Econ Assoc:37–41

DeFond LM, Raghunandan K, Subramanyam KR (2002) Do non-audit services fees impair auditor independence? Evidence from going concern audit opinions. J Account Res 40(4):1247–1274

Elliott R, Highfield M, Schaub M (2006) Contagion or competition: going concern audit opinions for real estate firms. J Real Estate Finan Econ 32(4):435–448

Fargher NL, Jiang L (2008) Changes in the audit environment and auditors' propensity to issue going-concern opinions. Audit A J Pract 27(2):55–77. https://doi.org/10.2308/aud.2008.27.2.55

Feldmann D, Read WJ (2013) Going-concern audit opinions for bankrupt companies – impact of credit rating. Manag Audit J 28(4):345–363. https://doi.org/10.1108/02686901311311936

Feng M, Li C (2014) Are auditors professionally skeptical? evidence from auditors' going-concern opinions and management earnings forecasts. J Account Res 52(5):1061–1085. https://doi.org/10.1111/1475-679X.12064

Ference SB (2015) All CPAs should be concerned about going concern. J Account 219(2):20–21

Firth M (1978) Qualified audit reports: their impact on investment decisions. Account Rev 53(3):642–650

Firth M (2002) Auditor-provided consultancy services and their associations with audit fees and audit opinions. J Bus Finan Account 29(5–6):661–693

Firth M, Mo LLP, Wong RMK (2014) Auditors' reporting conservatism after regulatory sanctions: evidence from China. J Int Account Res 13(2):1–24. https://doi.org/10.2308/jiar-50711

Fleak SK, Wilson ER (1994) The incremental information content of the going-concern audit opinion. J Account Audit Finan 9(1):149–166

Foster BP, Ward TJ, Woodroof J (1998) An analysis of the usefulness of debt defaults and going concern opinions in bankruptcy risk assessment. J Account Audit Finan 13(3):351–371. https://doi.org/10.1177/0148558X9801300311

Gaeremynck A, Willekens M (2003) The endogenous relationship between audit-report type and business termination: evidence on private firms in a non-litigious environment. Account Bus Res (Wolters Kluwer UK) 33(1):65–79

Gallizo JL, Saladrigues R (2016) An analysis of determinants of going concern audit opinion: Evidence from Spain stock exchange. Intang Cap 12(1):1–16. https://doi.org/10.3926/ic.683

Garcia-Blandon J, Argiles-Bosch JM (2017): The interaction effects of firm and partner tenure on audit quality. Account Bus Res :1–21 doi:10.1080/00014788.2017.1289073

Geiger MA, Raghunandan K (2002) Going-concern opinions in the "new" legal environment. Account Horizons 16(1):17–26. https://doi.org/10.2308/acch.2002.16.1.17

Geiger MA, Raghunandan K, Riccardi W (2014) The global financial crisis: U.S. bankruptcies and going-concern audit opinions. Account Horizons 28(1):59–75. Doi:10.2308/acch-50659

Geiger MA, Rama DV (2006) Audit firm size and going-concern reporting accuracy. Account Horizons 20(1):1–17

Ho JL (1994) The effect of experience on consensus of going-concern judgments. Behav Res Account 6:160–177

Holder-Webb LM, Wilkin MS (2000) The incremental information content of SAS no. 59 going-concern opinions. J Account Res 38(1):209–219. https://doi.org/10.2307/2672929

Hope O-K, Langli JC (2010) Auditor independence in a private firm and low litigation risk setting. Account Rev 85(2):573–605

Hopwood W, McKeown JC, Mutchler JF (1994) A reexamination of auditor versus model accuracy within the context of the going-concern opinion decision. Contemp Account Res 10 (2):409–431. https://doi.org/10.1111/j.1911-3846.1994.tb00400.x

Hsu J, Young W, Chu C (2011) Price behavior of qualified companies around the audit report and report announcement days: The case of Taiwan. J Int Finan Manag Account 22(2):114–130. https://doi.org/10.1111/j.1467-646X.2011.01047.x

Ianniello G, Galloppo G (2015) Stock market reaction to auditor opinions—Italian evidence. Manag Audit J 30(6/7):610–632

Ireland JC (2003) An empirical investigation of determinants of audit reports in the UK. J Bus Financ Account 30(7/8):975–1016. https://doi.org/10.1111/1468-5957.05417

Jones FL (1996) The information content of the auditor's going concern evaluation. J Account Public Policy 15(1):1–27. https://doi.org/10.1016/0278-4254(95)00062-3

Kao JL, Yan L, Wenjun Z (2014) Did SOX influence the association between fee dependence and auditors' propensity to issue going-concern opinions? Audit A J Pract Theory 33(2):165–185

Kaplan SE, Williams DD (2013) Do going concern audit reports protect auditors from litigation? a simultaneous equations approach. Account Rev 88(1):199–232. https://doi.org/10.2308/accr-50279

Kausar A, Taffler RJ, Tan CEL (2017) Legal regimes and investor response to the auditor's going-concern opinion. J Account Audit Finan 32(1):40–72

Khan SA, Lobo G, Nwaeze ET (2017) Public re-release of going-concern opinions and market reaction. Account Bus Res 47(3):237–267

Knechel WR, Vanstraelen A (2007) The relationship between auditor tenure and audit quality implied by going concern opinions. Audit A J Pract Theory 26(1):113–131. https://doi.org/10.2308/aud.2007.26.1.113

Krishnan GP, Changjiang W (2015) The relation between managerial ability and audit fees and going concern opinions. Audit A J Pract Theory 34(3):139–160

Krishnan J, Raghunandan K, Yang JS (2007) Were former andersen clients treated more leniently than other clients? evidence from going-concern modified audit opinions. Account Horizons 21 (4):423–435

Krishnan J, Stephens R (1995) Evidence on opinion shopping from audit opinion conservatism. J Account Public Policy 14(3):179–201. https://doi.org/10.1016/0278-4254(95)00020-F

Laitinen EK, Laitinen T (1998) Qualified audit reports in Finland: evidence from large companies. Eur Account Rev 7(4):639–653

Lam K, Mensah YM (2006) Auditors' decision-making under going concern uncertainties in low litigation risk environments: Evidence from Hong Kong. J Account Public Policy 25(6):706–739. https://doi.org/10.1016/j.jaccpubpol.2006.09.004

LaSalle RE, Anandarajan A (1996) Going concern uncertainties: disclaimer of opinion versus unqualified opinion with modified wording. Audit A J Pract Theory 15(2):29–48

LaSalle RE, Anandarajan A (1997) Bank loan officers' reactions to audit reports issued to entities with litigation and going concern uncertainties. Account Horizons 11(2):33–40

Lennox C (2000) Do companies successfully engage in opinion shopping? Evidence from the U.K. J Account Econ 29(3):321–337

Lennox CS (1999) The accuracy and the incremental information content of audit reports in predicting bankruptcy. J Bus Financ Account 26:757–778

Li C (2009) Does client importance affect auditor independence at the office level? Empirical evidence from going-concern opinions. Contemp Account Res 26(1):201–230. https://doi.org/10.1506/car.26.1.7

Louwers TJ (1998) The relation between going-concern opinions and the auditor's loss function. J Account Res 36(1):143–156

Maers MD, Maher MA, Giacomino DE (2003) Going-concern opinions: broadening the expectations gap. CPA J 73(10):38–42

Martin RD (2000) Going-concern uncertainty disclosures and conditions: a comparison of French, German, and U.S. practices. J Int Account Audit Tax 9(2):137–158. doi:10.1016/S1061-9518 (00)00029-X

Matsumura EM, Subramanyam KR, Tucker RR (1997) Strategic auditor behaviour and going-concern decisions. J Bus Finan Account 24(6):727–758. https://doi.org/10.1111/1468-5957.00131

Mayew WJ, Sethuraman M, Venkatachalam M (2015) MD&A disclosure and the firm's ability to continue as a going concern. Account Rev 90(4):1621–1651

Menon M, Williams DD (2010) Investor reaction to going concern audit reports. Account Rev 85 (6):2075–2105. https://doi.org/10.2308/accr.2010.85.6.2075

Mo PLL, Rui OM, Wu X (2015) Auditors' going concern reporting in the pre- and post-bankruptcy law eras: Chinese affiliates of Big 4 versus local auditors. Int J Account 50 (1):1–30. https://doi.org/10.1016/j.intacc.2014.12.005

Mutchler JF (1985) A multivariate analysis of the auditor's going-concern opinion decision. J Account Res 23(2):668–682. https://doi.org/10.2307/2490832

Mutchler JF (1986) Empirical evidence regarding the auditor's going-concern opinion decision. Audit A J Pract Theory 6(1):148

Mutchler JF, Williams DD (1990) The relationship between audit technology, client risk profiles, and the going-concern opinion decision. Audit A J Pract Theory 9(3):39–54

Myers L, Schmidt J, Wilkins M (2014) An investigation of recent changes in going concern reporting decisions among Big N and non-Big N auditors. Rev Quant Finan Account 43 (1):155–172. https://doi.org/10.2139/ssrn.1411316

Nogler GE (1995) The resolution of auditor going concern opinions. Audit A J Pract Theory 14 (2):54–73

O'Clock P, Devine K (1995) An investigation of framing and firm size on the auditor's going concern decision. Account Bus Res (Wolters Kluwer UK) 25(99):197–207. https://doi.org/10.1080/00014788.1995.9729942

Ogneva M, Subramanyam KR (2007) Does the stock market underreact to going concern opinions? Evidence from the U.S. and Australia. J Account Econ 43(2/3):439–452

Pucheta-Martínez MC, Martínez AV, Benau MAG (2004) Reactions of the Spanish capital market to qualified audit reports. Eur Account Rev 13(4):689–711

Quick R, Warming-Rasmussen B (2015) An experimental analysis of the effects of non-audit services on auditor independence in appearance in the European Union: evidence from Germany. J Int Finan Manag Account 26(2):150–187

Rau SE, Moser DV (1999) Does Performing Other audit tasks affect going-concern judgments? Account Rev 74(4):493. https://doi.org/10.1016/j.jacceco.2006.12.004

Read WJ (2015) Auditor fees and going-concern reporting decisions on bankrupt companies: additional evidence. Curr Issues Audit 9(1):A13–A27. https://doi.org/10.2308/ciia-51109

Read WJ, Yezegel A (2016) Auditor tenure and going concern opinions for bankrupt clients: additional evidence. Audit A J Pract Theory 35(1):163–179

Robinson D (2008) Auditor independence and auditor-provided tax service: evidence from going-concern audit opinions prior to bankruptcy filings. Audit A J Pract Theory 27(2):31–54. https://doi.org/10.2308/aud.2008.27.2.31

Ruiz -Barbadillo E, Gomez-Aguilar N, Biedma-Lopez E (2006) Long-term audit engagements and opinion shopping: Spanish evidence, Account Forum. 30:61–79. doi:10.1016/j.accfor.2005.03.007

Ruiz-Barbadillo E, Gomez NA, De Fuentes C, García MB (2004) Audit quality and the going concern decision making process: Spanish evidence. Eur Account Rev:597–620

Ruiz-Barbadillo E, Gomez-Aguilar N, Carrera N (2009) Does mandatory audit firm rotation enhance auditor independence? Evidence from Spain. Audit A J Pract Theory 28(1):113–135. https://doi.org/10.2308/aud.2009.28.1.113

Ryu TG, Roh CJ (2007) The auditor's going-concern opinion decision. Int J Bus Econ 6(2):89–101

Schaub M (2006) Investor overreaction to going concern audit opinion announcements. Appl Finan Econ 16:1163–1170

Seipel C, Tunnell L (1995) An empirical investigation into the relationship between "subject to" going concern opinions and risk shifts. Am Bus Rev 13(2):1–5

Shirata CY, Sakagami M (2008) An analysis of the "going concern assumption": text mining from Japanese financial reports. J Emerg Technol Account 5:1–16. https://doi.org/10.2308/jeta.2008.5.1.1

Soltani B (2000) Some empirical evidence to support the relationship between audit reports and stock prices—the French case. Int J Audit 4(3):269–291. https://doi.org/10.1111/1099-1123.00317

Taffler RJ, Lu J, Kausar A (2004) In denial? Stock market underreaction to going-concern audit report disclosures. J Account Econ 38:263–296

Ting W, Yen SH, Chiu CL (2008) The influence of qualified foreign institutional investors on the association between default risk and audit opinions: evidence from the Chinese stock market. Authors J Compil 16(5):400–415. https://doi.org/10.1111/j.1467-8683.2008.00699.x

Tsipouridou M, Spathis C (2013) Audit opinion and earnings management: evidence from Greece. Account Forum 38(1):38–54

Tucker RR, Matsumura EM, Subramanyam KR (2003) Going-concern judgments: an experimental test of the self-fulfilling prophecy and forecast accuracy. J Account Public Policy 22(5):401–432

Vandenbogaerde S, Renderes A, Willekens M (2011) Expected client loss and auditor independence: a partner-Level analysis in a low litigious setting. Research Center Accountancy, Leuven

Vanstraelen A (2003) Going-concern opinions, auditor switching, and the self-fulfilling prophecy effect examined in the regulatory context of Belgium. J Account Audit Finan 18:231–253

Venuti EK (2004) The going-concern assumption revisited: assessing a company's future viability. CPA J 74(5):40–43

Vermeer TE, Raghunandan K, Forgione DA (2013) Going-concern modified audit opinions for non-profit organizations. J Public Budgeting, Account Finan Manag 25(1):113–134

Weiss MD (2002) The worsening crisis of confidence on Wall Street: the role of auditing firms. http://www.weissratings.com/worsening-crisis.pdf

Wertheim P, Fowler WE (2005) Audit firm differences in the issuance of going concern opinions prior to client bankruptcy. J Account Finan Res 13(5):93–109

Wu CY-H, Hsu H-H, Haslam J (2016) Audit committees, non-audit services, and auditor reporting decisions prior to failure. Br Account Rev 48(2):240–256

Xu Y, Carson E, Fargher N, Jiang L (2013) Responses by Australian auditors to the global financial crisis. Account Fin 53(1):301–338. https://doi.org/10.1111/j.1467-629X.2011.00459.x

Yeh C-C, Chi D, Lin Y (2014) Going-concern prediction using hybrid random forests and rough set approach. Inf Sci 254:98–110

Young A, Wang Y (2010) Multi-risk level examination of going concern modifications. Manag Audit J 25(8):756–791. https://doi.org/10.1108/02686901011069542

# Chapter 3
# Effects of GCOs in Italy: Some Empirical Evidence

**Abstract** The literature related with financial reporting events (such as earnings forecast, annual reports releases, financial plan, takeover, merger announcements etc.) is controversial. The main issue arises to confirm whether and to what extent those events affect stock market returns. As regards audit reports release and their impact on the stock market, many studies attempted overtime to capture the magnitude of these phenomena. This chapter aims at exploring the same phenomenon. I use the Event Study methodology (ES) to test whether GCOs impact on stock returns of firms listed at the Italian stock exchange, from 2008 to 2014, alongside the financial crisis. Findings are partially in line with previous studies shedding a light on the negative impact of GCOs on stock market returns, signalling a certain degree of value relevance. The main novelty is that Italian investors reacted (on average) negatively even when GCOs are attached to clean opinions. According to Carson et al (Audit A J Pract Theory 32(1):353–384, 2013) categorization, this research falls in full among studies aimed at detecting consequences of GCOs for shareholders. Moreover, the location matter of the study seems particularly useful because only another study (Ianniello and Galloppo in Manag Audit J 30(6/7):610–632, 2015) has detected the impact of GCOs on stock market returns in Italy.

## 3.1 Previous Studies and Investigation Purposes

In Italy, legislative decree no. 39/2010 and subsequent laws have definitely pushed the auditing process toward an international perspective. Several provisions, such as the mandatory full adoption of International Auditing Standards (ISAs), and other fulfilments, have been introduced.

In this respect, Ianniello and Galloppo (2015) showed that, on average, the qualifications expressed in the audit reports containing a GCO of the Italian listed companies had negative effects on the respective stock prices. At the same time, they highlighted that unmodified opinions containing a GCO positively affect stock

© The Author(s), under exclusive licence to Springer International Publishing AG, part of Springer Nature 2018
S. Brunelli, *Audit Reporting for Going Concern Uncertainty*,
SpringerBriefs in Accounting, https://doi.org/10.1007/978-3-319-73046-2_3

prices. Using the ES, they analysed a data set covering 2007–2010, containing 97 observations from 41 unique firms.

Starting from the pioneering work of Ianniello and Galloppo (2015) related to the Italian context, the effects of modified/unmodified opinions containing an emphasis of matter paragraph related to GC on the stock market deserve further empirical investigation, for at least two reasons:

1. to confirm their results with respect to time, by observing stock market reactions for a longer period;
2. to assess whether the persistent effect of a GCO on stock market prices (if it exists) has represented one of the reason to foster the ISA 570 revision.

I therefore analyse a sample of 248 Italian listed firms, excluding banks and insurance firms, for the period 2008–2014 adopting ES and using different statistical tests. The main goal is to test whether the effect of GCOs exists, in what direction and to what extent it affects stock prices. Indeed, the presence of a GC-effect might demonstrate its relevance with respect to the firm market capitalisation, at least around the issuance of the audit report. This analysis is useful to assist regulators, auditors and standard setters for the further development of standards. Indeed, a positive or negative effect on stock prices could suggest a deeper fine-tuning of the standards, over time. On the other hand, a null effect could suggest the need to supersede on this issue, and to strive for improvements on other relevant questions related to the complex area of auditing, at least with regard to the Italian context.

Over time, many international studies have tried to investigate whether specific events that happened to listed firms might determine stock market reactions. The literature in this field can be classified, according to the adopted methodology, period under investigation, analysed country and other relevant aspects. Craswell (1985) identified two main types of studies: the "efficient market test" which uses the market model to estimate parameters for individual securities, testing changes in average returns, and "experimental studies" based on simulations. In regard to the first group, Holt and Moizer (1990) define "reaction studies" as those analysing the entire audit process until the release of the audit report and stakeholders' reactions. This type of research has been broken down into studies examining individuals' behaviour using laboratory experiments, and studies analysing market model residuals after the release of a qualified audit opinion. Tahinakis and Samarinas (2016) adopt this categorisation too. They call the first group "experimental-based studies" and the second one "market-based studies". The latter is mainly based on ES and abnormal returns.

Several studies, grounded on "market based studies", have been conducted (Al-Thuneibat et al. 2008; Ameen et al. 1994; Dodd et al. 1984; Firth 1978; Pucheta-Martínez et al. 2004), which conclude that audit opinions have no significant effects on stock prices. Conversely, other scholars show that only certain types of audit opinions have an impact on stock prices (Chow and Rice 1982; Dopuch et al. 1986; Soltani 2000).

Referring to "market-based studies", Ittonen (2012) identified two types of window approaches: the short event window approach (Al-Thuneibat et al. 2008; Baskin 1972; Chen and Church 1996; Davis 1982; Firth 1978; Ianniello and Galloppo 2015; Pucheta-Martínez et al. 2004; Soltani 2000) and the long event window approach (Chow and Rice 1982; Elliott 1982; Ogneva and Subramanyam 2007; Taffler et al. 2004). The first group of studies assumes that stock markets are efficient and new information (bad or good news) has an effect on stock prices at and immediately after the announcement. Differently, the long event window approach implies that investors need time to make a decision, and interpret bad news. Anyway, the results for both categories are contradictory and various, depending on the sample, time under investigation and other specific factors.

It is worth remarking that contradictory results in the literature could be primarily due to the differences in auditing and accounting practices.

As known, audit opinions are primarily distinguished as follows:

1. unmodified (also called unqualified) opinions;
2. modified opinions.

For the purpose of this work, and in accordance with the reviewed literature, it is useful to further divide opinions belonging to the first category into three subgroups:

    1a clean audit opinions;
    1b opinions with an emphasis of matter paragraph related to GC;
    1c opinions with other matter paragraphs.

Similarly, among the opinions belonging to the second category we can distinguish two subgroups:

    2a those (qualified or except for, adverse opinion and disclaimer of opinion) with a paragraph related to GCO;
    2b those (qualified or except for, adverse opinion and disclaimer of opinion) with other matter paragraphs.

With the aim of providing additional insights to the debate related to GCO—Stock Market Reaction, I primarily focus on subgroups 1b and 2a as shown in Fig. 3.1.

I analysed audit reports of all Italian listed firms, excluding banks and insurance companies, during the period 2008–2014. Years covered by the analysis encompass the financial crisis and reach the eve of ISA 570 revision.

According to Ianniello and Galloppo (2015), even though the period and sample investigated are partially the same, I assume that an effect on share prices exists. On the other hand, I go beyond their results, checking whether the evidence they found is confirmed. It is worth noting that when the effect on share prices is revealed, its magnitude and direction is a function of the opinion types included in the sample.

Thus, if the majority of opinions containing a GCO are modified, it is reasonable to find a negative effect. For this reason it is meaningful to test if the negative effect

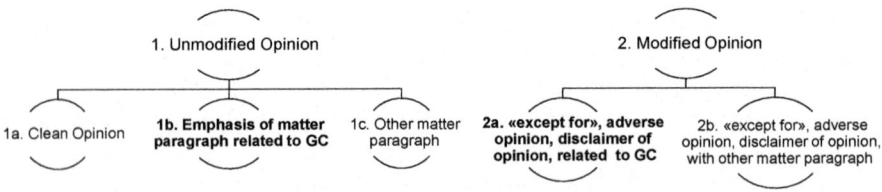

**Fig. 3.1** Types of audit opinions. *Source* Author elaboration *Notes* Audit opinions categorisation adopted by the ISA's, focusing in particular on GC (Going Concern). In the study, the attention was focused on subgroups 1b and 2a

persists if only unmodified opinions containing a GCO are encompassed in the sample. In this way, the potential GCO's effects are better isolated.

Summing up, in the following paragraphs, I test the hypothesis according to the presence of GCOs affecting negatively the stock market, as revealed by the abnormal returns of stock prices in the days before, on the event date and in the days after the annual report's issuance.

## 3.2  Data Sample Description

I analysed audit reports on separate and consolidated financial statements, but only included observations extrapolated from consolidated annual reports and separate financial statements when the consolidated account was not available. The data set used for the analysis was gathered from different sources: stock market prices (the main Italian stock market index, FTSE MIB); the ratios used for the sample description were retrieved from Datastream; while audit reports were collected by downloading the firm's annual reports from their official websites. The period covered goes from 2008 to 2014 (fiscal years). The sample selection started by considering any newly listed or delisted firms in the period under investigation. In this way, all the listed companies, even those listed for only one year during the time span, were investigated.

Starting from a potential sample of 2067 firms/observations, I excluded banks and insurance companies because the structure of the accounting information and financial statements is different from the industrial sector. Then, I removed companies with missing opinions. In this way, the total sample dropped to 1556 firms/observations.

To classify the audit opinions, I used the categorisation established by ISA 700. Preliminarily, I separated those containing a GCO from those not containing a GCO. During this phase, I found firms for which some data were missing (such as availability of market share, or unreliable stock return data). At the end, the total clean sample is composed of 1437 firms/observations. The majority of observations

**Table 3.1** Sample's breakdown

| Number of listed companies | | 2008 | 2009 | 2010 | 2011 | 2012 | 2013 | 2014 | Total observations |
|---|---|---|---|---|---|---|---|---|---|
| | | 300 | 296 | 296 | 304 | 296 | 290 | 285 | 2067 |
| Removed firms | | (65) | (59) | (60) | (68) | (69) | (64) | (72) | (457) |
| Sample selection | | **235** | **237** | **236** | **236** | **227** | **226** | **213** | **1610** |
| Missing opinions | | (6) | (10) | (10) | (9) | (8) | (5) | (6) | (54) |
| Remaining firms | | 229 | 227 | 226 | 227 | 219 | 221 | 207 | 1556 |
| no GCO | Unmodified opinion | 175 | 173 | 169 | 166 | 156 | 161 | 156 | 1156 |
| | Unmodified opinion with general emphasis of matter | 22 | 23 | 18 | 24 | 17 | 17 | 17 | 138 |
| | Qualified opinion "Except for" | 3 | 3 | 2 | 1 | 0 | 0 | 0 | 9 |
| | Disclaimer of opinion | 1 | 0 | 0 | 0 | 1 | 0 | 1 | 3 |
| | Total | 201 | 199 | 189 | 191 | 174 | 178 | 174 | 1306 |
| Other missing data (from not GCO) | | (16) | (17) | (14) | (16) | (12) | (13) | (14) | (102) |
| Final sample analysed (not GCO)—number of firms | | **185** | **182** | **175** | **175** | **162** | **165** | **160** | **1204** |
| Number of companies receiving types of opinion | | | | | | | | | |
| GCO | (a) Unmodified with an emphasis of matter paragraph related to going concern | 24 | 16 | 25 | 22 | 32 | 30 | 24 | 173 |
| | (b) Qualified opinion "Except for" | 0 | 3 | 3 | 2 | 0 | 0 | 1 | 9 |
| | (c) Disclaimer of opinion | 4 | 8 | 8 | 12 | 13 | 13 | 8 | 66 |
| | (d) Adverse opinion | 0 | 1 | 1 | 0 | 0 | 0 | 0 | 2 |
| | Total | 28 | 28 | 37 | 36 | 45 | 43 | 33 | 250 |
| Other missing data (from GCO) | | (0) | (1) | (2) | (2) | (4) | (6) | (2) | (17) |
| Final sample analysed (GCO)—number of firms | | **28** | **27** | **35** | **34** | **41** | **37** | **31** | **233** |
| Total final sample after the elimination of the other missing data | | | | | | | | | **1437** |

*Source* Author elaboration

*Notes* The table shows the sample logic from the beginning available firms/observations to the final sample used for the analysis (n = 1204, 83.78%) did not receive a GCO. Hence, only 233 observations (16.2%) contain a GCO. Among the latter, 77 contain severe modifications (except for, adverse opinion and disclaimer of opinion), representing 33% of the subsample related to GCOs. The remaining 156 observations refer to clean opinions with an emphasis of matter paragraph related to GC. The breakdown of the sample, by year and type of audit opinion, is provided in Table 3.1.

Analysing the sample composition, I can conclude that auditors, when financial troubles are expected in the near future, foster the formulation of a disclaimer of opinion rather than an adverse opinion. Indeed, the latter could hardly be seen as a case to recover and dangerous, at least, for the minority shareholders.

Considering that firms receiving GCO present, by definition, a certain degree of financial distress (even in the cases related to unmodified opinions containing a GCO), I choose financial statement items and ratios mainly related to GC, in accordance with Carson et al. (2013), Taffler et al. (2004). Not surprisingly, the Italian listed firms show, on average, a low or medium market capitalisation (SIZE mean = 54,9 million) and a negative Net Income (NI mean = −400,7 million €). The sample presents high variability in terms of total assets, equity, net income and net sales. In line with financial distress definition, it is worth highlighting the average negative Return on Assets (ROA mean = −11.7%) and the average high leverage (LEV mean = 548.9 million €). It is also important to consider that almost all the observations are related to firms that in the given year showed a net loss (89.7%) (Table 3.2).

**Table 3.2** Sample descriptive statistics (n = 233)

| Variable | Mean | Standard deviation | Median | Minimum | Maximum |
|---|---|---|---|---|---|
| TA | 2.891,09 | 5.083,43 | 1.317,38 | 0,46 | 37.539,21 |
| SIZE | 54,89 | 97,38 | 25,46 | 1,40 | 935,64 |
| NI | −400,68 | 1.417,21 | −139,73 | −17.937,60 | 2.052,53 |
| EQ | 116,93 | 1.413,90 | 100,06 | −13.429,07 | 6.491,00 |
| Net Sales | 1.887,59 | 4.191,86 | 661,93 | 0,01 | 26.739,00 |
| ROA (%) | −11,72 | 20,55 | −5,34 | −191,07 | 17,31 |
| LEV (%) | 548,89 | 2.333,15 | 130,04 | −7.767,84 | 20.526,84 |
| Current ratio | 0,99 | 0,98 | 0,83 | 0,08 | 10,30 |

*Source* Author elaboration

*Notes* Variables definition: TA, total assets in € million; SIZE, market capitalisation in € million; NI, net income in € million; EQ, Equity, in € million; Net Sales, sales in € million; ROA, return on assets (net income/Average total assets) in percentage; LEV, leverage (debt/Common equity) in percentage; Current ratio (Current Assets/Current Liabilities). Data for descriptive statistics elaboration were gathered from Datastream

## 3.3 The Event Study Methodology (ES): A Simple Way to Detect Complex Phenomena

As previously specified, via ES and related statistical tests, the dynamics of listed firms' stock prices at and around the release of audit reports are analysed. The main idea is that the magnitude of abnormal returns, at the time of the release of audit reports, might provide a measure of the impact of these events on the wealth of firms' claimholders (see Campbell et al. 1997 and reference therein for a complete survey on ES). In particular, I also test those effects in the light of new regulations introduced by some ISA amendments and revisions.

At the same time, ES allows me to test the Italian stock market efficiency since abnormal stock returns different from zero and persisting after the release of an audit report, are inconsistent with market efficiency (Fama 1991).

As in classical ES, I mainly analyse the behaviour of returns for a sample of Italian listed firms who received, in the period 2008–2014, a GCO in their audit reports. These types of events are mainly clustered in the period from the beginning of March to the end of June. The time displacement of the considered events should preserve the hypothesis of cross-sectional independence underlying the ES, since the event date is not common to all the firms in the sample. Anyway, since I found evidence of autocorrelation in the series, I performed others additional tests aimed at overriding the problem.

### 3.3.1 Design and Statistical Tests

To compute the Abnormal Returns (ARs) I compare, for each firm $i$, the observed daily log-returns with the expected ones which are estimated by using the classical linear market model:

$$R_{it} = \alpha_i + \beta_i RMt + \varepsilon_{it}, \quad \varepsilon_{it} \sim N(0, \sigma_i^2), \quad t \in EP \tag{3.1}$$

where $R_{it}$ is the return of firm $i$, observed at time $t$; $R_{Mt}$ is the Italian stock market index (FTSE MIB) and $\alpha_i$, $\beta_i \in R$ are parameters estimated over a period of "normal behaviour", i.e. the Estimation Period (EP) starting 200 days before the event date and ending 15 days after.

Let $t = 0$ represents the event date, ARs are then estimated in the Test Period which is set equal to 30 trading days around each event, $\mathbf{TP} = [-\mathbf{15}, \mathbf{0}) \bigcup (\mathbf{0}, +\mathbf{15}]$, and then divided into several subintervals. In particular, we focus on the following windows: $[-\mathbf{15}; -\mathbf{10})$; $(-\mathbf{2}, +\mathbf{2})$; $(+\mathbf{2}; +\mathbf{15}]$ and $[-\mathbf{1}, \mathbf{1}]$. The first three windows are further split into $[-\mathbf{15}; -\mathbf{2})$; $(-\mathbf{10}; -\mathbf{5})$; $(-\mathbf{5}, -\mathbf{1})$; $(+\mathbf{1}, +\mathbf{5})$; $(+\mathbf{5}, +\mathbf{10})$; $(+\mathbf{10}, +\mathbf{15}]$, while the latter into $(-\mathbf{1}, \mathbf{0})$; $(\mathbf{0})$; $(\mathbf{0}, +\mathbf{1})$ for a fine-tuning analysis in proximity of the event date. These windows are tied to our willingness to check, not only whether the disclosure of audit reports impacts on stock prices, but also if the market anticipates (or not) the release of the auditor's opinions.

For each stock $i$, ARs are defined as the difference between the observed returns around the day of the event, $t = 0$, and the return predicted by the market model in (3.1):

$$AR_{it} = R_{it} - \left( \hat{\alpha}_i + \hat{\beta}_i R_{Mt} \right) \quad t \in TP \tag{3.2}$$

where $\hat{\alpha}'_i s$ and $\hat{\beta}'_i s$ are the estimated parameters of the model for each firm i.

In other words, $AR'_{it}s$ measure the difference between the conditional returns on the event and the expected unconditional returns on the event. In so doing, abnormal returns might also highlight the change in wealth of the stockholder related to the event.

To perform the analysis for verifying whether or not the audit reports release impacts on stock prices ($H_0$: there are no ARs within the time period TP; $H_1$: presence of ARs within the TP), first the cross-sectional means of ARs are computed for each $t \in TP$:

$$\overline{AR}_t = \frac{1}{N} \sum_{i=1}^{N} AR_{it}, \tag{3.3}$$

with N representing the number of firms included in the sample.

Then, the cross-sectional mean of the Cumulative Abnormal Returns, $\overline{CAR}_{t_a t_b}$ are computed over each subinterval, $(t_a, t_b) \in TP$:

$$\overline{CAR}_{t_a t_b} = \sum_{t=t_a}^{t_b} \overline{AR}_t. \tag{3.4}$$

Within the Cross-Sectional Test (CST), the test statistic used for testing $H_0$: $\overline{CAR}_{t_a t_b} = 0$ is:

$$T^{CST}_{\overline{CAR}_{t_a t_b}} = \sqrt{N} \frac{\overline{CAR}_{t_a t_b}}{\sigma_{\overline{CAR}_{t_a t_b}}}, \tag{3.5}$$

where: $\sigma_{\overline{CAR}_{t_1 t_2}} = \sqrt{\frac{1}{N-1} \sum_{i=1}^{N} \left( CAR_{i,t_a t_b} - \overline{CAR}_{t_a t_b} \right)}$ and $CAR_{i,t_a t_b} = \sum_{t=t_a}^{t_b} AR_{i,t}$.

$T^{CST}_{\overline{CAR}_{t_a t_b}}$ is distributed as Student-T, and approximated to standard distribution for the big sample.

It is helpful to point out that the CST has a low power since it is particularly sensitive to disclosure-induced volatility which might lead to severe bias in abnormal returns (Brown and Warner 1985, 1980). Because of this drawback, the Crude Dependent Test (CDT) is also performed. CDT uses the variance of ARs in the whole EP and does not consider the variances across the windows in the TP.

The test statistic for testing the $H_0$ is:

$$T^{CD}_{\overline{CAR}_{t_a t_b}} = \frac{\overline{CAR}_{t_1 t_2}}{\sqrt{T_{EP}} . \sigma_{\overline{AR}_{EP}}} \tag{3.6}$$

where $T_{EP}$ is the length of the EP and $\sigma_{\overline{AR}_{EP}} = \sqrt{\frac{1}{(N-2)} \sum_{t_{EP}=1}^{T} \left( \varepsilon_{it_{EP}} - \overline{\varepsilon}_{t_{EP}} \right)^2}$, with $\overline{\varepsilon}_{t_{EP}} = \frac{1}{N} \sum_{N=1}^{N} \varepsilon_{i,t_{EP}}$.

Since, the series of abnormal returns in the sample are also characterized also by a certain degree of skewness, the Skewness Corrected Test (SCT) is applied to obtain reliable results. To test the null hypothesis, the most appropriate test statistic in the presence of skewed abnormal return distributions (asymptotically standard normal distributed) is:

$$T_{\overline{CAR}_{t_a t_b}}^{SCT} = \sqrt{N} \left[ \sigma_{t_a t_b} + \frac{1}{3} \gamma \sigma_{t_a t_b}^2 + \frac{1}{27} \gamma^2 \sigma_{t_a t_b}^3 + \frac{1}{6N} \gamma \right] \tag{3.7}$$

where: $\sigma_{t_a t_b} = \frac{\overline{CAR}_{t_a t_b}}{\sigma_{\overline{CAR}_{t_a t_b}}}$, $\sigma_{\overline{CAR}_{t_a t_b}} = \sqrt{\frac{1}{N-1} \sum_{i=1}^{N} \left( CAR_{i,t_a t_b} - \overline{CAR}_{t_a t_b} \right)^2}$

and $\gamma = \frac{N}{(N-2)(N-1)} \sum_{i=1}^{N} \left( CAR_{i,t_a t_b} - \overline{CAR}_{t_a t_b} \right)^3 \left( \sigma_{\overline{CAR}_{t_a t_b}} \right)^{-3}$

To obtain more robust results, I also apply the Mikkelson and Partch test (MP) (1988) in which a factor for each company of the sample is applied to correct the bias induced by the presence of serial correlation in the returns:

$$Z_{\overline{CAR}_{t_a t_b}}^{MP} = \frac{1}{\sqrt{N}} \sum_{i=1}^{N} \left[ CAR_{i,t_a t_b} \middle/ \sqrt{\sigma_{CAR_{i,t_a t_b}}^2} \right]^{-3} \tag{3.8}$$

where $\sigma_{CAR_{i,t_a t_b}}^2 = \sigma_{\overline{AR}_{EP}}^2 \left[ T + \frac{T^2}{T_{EP}} + \frac{\sum_{t=t_a}^{t_b} R_{Mt} - T\left( \overline{R}_M \right)^2}{\sum_{t_{EP}=1}^{T_{EP}} \left( R_{Mt} - \overline{R}_M \right)^2} \right]$ is the variance of the cumulated prediction error of firm $i$, $\sigma_{\overline{AR}_{EP}}^2$ is the residual variance of the market model regression for *firm i*, $T = t_b - t_a + 1$ is the number of days in the window, $T_{EP}$ is the number of days in the period used to estimate the market model, $R_{Mt}$ is the market return at time t, and $\overline{R}_M$ is the average of market returns in the estimation period.

Notwithstanding its higher reliability, the MP test has been modified over time by scholars in order to correct for the cross-sectional correlation in abnormal returns. In this respect, Boehmer et al. (1991), Mentz and Schiereck (2008), Kolari and Pynnönen (2010) made relevant improvements. Firstly, (Mentz and Schiereck 2008) based on Boehmer et al. (1991) calculated SRi as:

$$SRi = CAR_{i,t_a t_b} \middle/ \sqrt{\sigma_{CAR_{i,t_a t_b}}^2} \tag{3.9}$$

and then, used (3.9) to calculate a Z statistic (called here $Z_M$):

$$Z_M = \frac{1}{N} \sum_{i=1}^{N} SRi \middle/ \sqrt{\frac{1}{N(N-1)} \sum_{i=1}^{N} \left( SRi - \sum_{i=1}^{N} \frac{SRi}{N} \right)^2} \tag{3.10}$$

Finally, Kolari and Pynnönen (2010) have proposed a new statistic test (hereafter MP corrected) that further modifies the one proposed by Boehmer et al. (1991) introducing $h = \sqrt{\frac{1-\bar{\rho}}{1+(N-1)\bar{\rho}}}$, which is a correction factor to the above defined $Z^M$ where $\bar{\rho}$ is the average of the sample cross correlations of the estimation period residuals, and N is the number of observations in the considered sample. This last test is the one used by the aforementioned Ianniello and Galloppo (2015) study.

## 3.4   How Italian Investors Reacted in the Period 2008–2014

For empirical investigation purposes, the total subsample related to audit reports containing a GCO has been further classified.

Given 233 firms/observations I assigned a series of alphabetical labels to distinguish among: emphasis of matter paragraph (a), except for (b), disclaimer of opinion (c) and adverse opinion (d). After that, I applied all the aforementioned statistic tests to develop ES for all categories as a whole (all GCOs), for each separately with the exception of adverse opinion (d) (I had only two firms/observations in the period investigated, see Table 3.1), and, finally, for the "bcd", which encompasses all the categories with the exception of the emphasis of matter paragraph. The latter category was created in order to distinguish the effects between modified opinions containing a GCO from unmodified opinions with an emphasis of matter paragraph related to GC. Table 3.3 shows the results of each test.

First, it is important to stress that, when the statistical tests are significant, I found a systematic negative impact of GCO on stock prices. The results corroborate those achieved by Ianniello and Galloppo (2015) with a relevant exception represented by the positive impact they found in reference to the emphasis of matter paragraph related to GC. This contradiction could be explained by the differences in the data set, covered period and firms/observations. Moreover, the persistence of the economic crises after 2010 could represent an effective explanation. In other words, an unmodified audit opinion with an emphasis of matter paragraph related to GC has shifted over time from good news to bad news, at least around the audit reports release. The CST-test shows that some pre-disclosure effects can be observed on the stock market regarding "disclaimer of opinion", "bcd" and "except for". Indeed, the results are statistically significant for different levels in the window $(-15; -2)$. In addition, results show that in the interval $(-2; +2)$, there are effects on stock prices for "all GCOs" and also for unmodified opinions containing a GCO. These results are further confirmed by all the sub windows around the audit report issuance $(-1; +1)$. It should be noted that post-announcement effects exist for all the events taken into account, except for the emphasis of matter paragraph related to GC.

**Table 3.3** Stock market's reaction to audit opinion

| Event window | All GCO (abcd) (n = 233) | | | Disclaimer of opinion (c) (n = 59) | | | (bcd) (n = 70) | | | Emphasis of matter paragraph related to GC (a) (n = 163) | | | Except for (b) (n = 9) | | |
|---|---|---|---|---|---|---|---|---|---|---|---|---|---|---|---|
| | T | p-value | | T | p-value | | T | p-value | | T | p-value | | T | p-value | |
| **(−15;−2)** | | | | | | | | | | | | | | | |
| CST | 0,47 | 0,680 | | −1,46 | 0,072 | * | −2,07 | 0,019 | ** | 1,89 | 0,971 | | −2,86 | 0,002 | *** |
| CDT | 0,47 | 0,681 | | −0,79 | 0,215 | | −1,16 | 0,123 | | 1,52 | 0,936 | | −0,30 | 0,384 | |
| SCT | 0,49 | 0,687 | | −1,48 | 0,069 | * | −2,08 | 0,019 | ** | 2,10 | 0,982 | | −2,19 | 0,014 | ** |
| MP | −1,41 | 0,160 | | −1,02 | 0,313 | | −1,72 | 0,089 | * | −0,55 | 0,580 | | −1,94 | 0,094 | ** |
| MP corrected | −0,78 | 0,437 | | −0,53 | 0,598 | | −0,93 | 0,357 | | −0,31 | 0,755 | | −1,83 | 0,109 | |
| **(−2; +2)** | | | | | | | | | | | | | | | |
| CST | −2,10 | 0,018 | ** | −0,92 | 0,180 | | −0,51 | 0,307 | | −2,34 | 0,010 | *** | 1,09 | 0,863 | |
| CDT | −2,04 | 0,021 | ** | −0,57 | 0,284 | | −0,34 | 0,367 | | −1,65 | 0,050 | ** | 0,25 | 0,599 | |
| SCT | −1,92 | 0,028 | ** | −0,74 | 0,228 | | −0,42 | 0,336 | | −2,26 | 0,012 | ** | 1,31 | 0,906 | |
| MP | −3,82 | 0,000 | *** | −1,22 | 0,229 | | −0,68 | 0,496 | | −4,12 | 0,000 | *** | 0,63 | 0,546 | |
| MP corrected | −2,04 | 0,043 | ** | −0,65 | 0,520 | | −0,36 | 0,721 | | −2,24 | 0,026 | ** | 0,35 | 0,733 | |
| **(+2; +15)** | | | | | | | | | | | | | | | |
| CST | −1,56 | 0,060 | * | −1,98 | 0,024 | ** | −2,82 | 0,002 | *** | 0,19 | 0,577 | | −3,41 | 0,000 | *** |
| CDT | −1,49 | 0,068 | * | −1,11 | 0,134 | | −1,71 | 0,043 | ** | 0,14 | 0,555 | | −0,62 | 0,269 | |
| SCT | −1,60 | 0,055 | * | −2,54 | 0,005 | *** | −3,70 | 0,000 | *** | 0,20 | 0,580 | | −3,80 | 0,000 | *** |
| MP | −2,72 | 0,007 | *** | −1,22 | 0,227 | | −1,80 | 0,077 | * | −2,07 | 0,040 | ** | −2,65 | 0,033 | ** |
| MP corrected | −1,46 | 0,145 | | 0,61 | 0,548 | | 0,50 | 0,616 | | −1,15 | 0,254 | | −0,73 | 0,490 | |
| **(0)** | | | | | | | | | | | | | | | |
| CST | −2,05 | 0,020 | ** | −1,06 | 0,146 | | −0,74 | 0,229 | | −2,22 | 0,013 | ** | 0,82 | 0,794 | |
| CDT | −2,03 | 0,021 | ** | −0,76 | 0,223 | | −0,57 | 0,285 | | −1,43 | 0,076 | * | 0,18 | 0,571 | |

(continued)

**Table 3.3** (continued)

| Event window | All GCO (abcd) (n = 233) | | Disclaimer of opinion (c) (n = 59) | | (bcd) (n = 70) | | Emphasis of matter paragraph related to GC (a) (n = 163) | | Except for (b) (n = 9) | |
|---|---|---|---|---|---|---|---|---|---|---|
| | T | p-value | T | p-value | T | p-value | T | p-value | T | p-value |
| SCT | -2,01 | 0,022 ** | -1,12 | 0,131 | -0,78 | 0,217 | -1,83 | 0,034 ** | 1,02 | 0,846 |
| MP | -3,39 | 0,001 *** | -1,04 | 0,302 | -0,84 | 0,405 | -3,50 | 0,001 *** | -0,33 | 0,752 |
| MP corrected | -1,89 | 0,060 * | -0,59 | 0,555 | -0,47 | 0,638 | -1,96 | 0,051 * | -0,18 | 0,864 |
| (-1; 0) | | | | | | | | | | |
| CST | -1,94 | 0,026 ** | -0,91 | 0,181 | -0,41 | 0,339 | -2,45 | 0,007 *** | 1,29 | 0,901 |
| CDT | -2,02 | 0,021 ** | -0,69 | 0,245 | -0,34 | 0,368 | -1,63 | 0,051 * | 0,34 | 0,635 |
| SCT | -1,99 | 0,023 ** | -0,94 | 0,173 | -0,43 | 0,334 | -2,55 | 0,005 *** | 1,43 | 0,923 |
| MP | -2,98 | 0,003 *** | -1,07 | 0,289 | -0,42 | 0,679 | -3,29 | 0,001 *** | 0,76 | 0,473 |
| MP corrected | -1,62 | 0,106 | -0,60 | 0,549 | -0,23 | 0,822 | -1,81 | 0,072 * | 0,37 | 0,721 |
| (0; +1) | | | | | | | | | | |
| CST | -1,45 | 0,073 * | -0,65 | 0,258 | -0,51 | 0,306 | -1,68 | 0,046 ** | 0,81 | 0,790 |
| CDT | -1,35 | 0,089 * | -0,47 | 0,319 | -0,39 | 0,350 | -0,94 | 0,174 | 0,15 | 0,560 |
| SCT | -1,35 | 0,088 * | -0,59 | 0,278 | -0,46 | 0,322 | -1,55 | 0,061 * | 1,03 | 0,849 |
| MP | -3,10 | 0,002 *** | -1,44 | 0,157 | -1,49 | 0,142 | -2,73 | 0,007 *** | -0,65 | 0,538 |
| MP corrected | -1,73 | 0,085 * | -0,82 | 0,416 | -0,85 | 0,396 | -1,51 | 0,134 | -0,41 | 0,692 |
| (-1; +1) | | | | | | | | | | |
| CST | -1,65 | 0,049 ** | -0,81 | 0,210 | -0,38 | 0,351 | -1,90 | 0,029 ** | 1,26 | 0,897 |
| CDT | -1,58 | 0,057 * | -0,51 | 0,306 | -0,26 | 0,397 | -1,28 | 0,101 | 0,30 | 0,618 |
| SCT | -1,57 | 0,058 * | -0,72 | 0,235 | -0,34 | 0,365 | -1,84 | 0,033 ** | 1,43 | 0,923 |
| MP | -3,40 | 0,001 *** | -1,49 | 0,142 | -1,17 | 0,247 | -3,30 | 0,001 *** | 0,27 | 0,793 |

(continued)

**Table 3.3** (continued)

| Event window | All GCO (abcd) (n = 233) | | | Disclaimer of opinion (c) (n = 59) | | | (bcd) (n = 70) | | | Emphasis of matter paragraph related to GC (a) (n = 163) | | | Except for (b) (n = 9) | | |
|---|---|---|---|---|---|---|---|---|---|---|---|---|---|---|---|
| | T | p-value | | T | p-value | | T | p-value | | T | p-value | | T | p-value | |
| MP corrected | −1,83 | 0,068 | * | −0,81 | 0,424 | | −0,63 | 0,534 | | −1,80 | 0,074 | * | 0,15 | 0,885 | |
| (−15; −10) | | | | | | | | | | | | | | | |
| CST | 1,60 | 0,945 | | −0,90 | 0,185 | | −1,45 | 0,074 | * | 2,38 | 0,991 | | −1,51 | 0,065 | * |
| CDT | 1,80 | 0,964 | | −0,40 | 0,343 | | −0,70 | 0,243 | | 2,37 | 0,991 | | −0,17 | 0,432 | |
| SCT | 1,70 | 0,955 | | −1,00 | 0,158 | | −1,32 | 0,094 | * | 2,73 | 0,997 | | −2,42 | 0,008 | *** |
| MP | −0,65 | 0,518 | | −0,13 | 0,896 | | −0,74 | 0,460 | | −0,29 | 0,775 | | −1,19 | 0,272 | |
| MP corrected | −0,37 | 0,709 | | −0,08 | 0,937 | | −0,09 | 0,929 | | −0,16 | 0,873 | | −1,01 | 0,346 | |
| (−10; −5) | | | | | | | | | | | | | | | |
| CST | −2,10 | 0,018 | ** | −1,83 | 0,033 | ** | −2,19 | 0,014 | ** | −0,93 | 0,177 | | −1,59 | 0,056 | * |
| CDT | −1,70 | 0,045 | ** | −0,93 | 0,176 | | −1,15 | 0,125 | | −0,57 | 0,284 | | −0,20 | 0,422 | |
| SCT | −2,07 | 0,019 | ** | −1,95 | 0,026 | ** | −2,01 | 0,022 | ** | −0,90 | 0,184 | | −2,55 | 0,005 | *** |
| MP | −3,13 | 0,002 | *** | −1,54 | 0,130 | | −1,72 | 0,090 | * | −2,61 | 0,010 | *** | −1,34 | 0,222 | |
| MP corrected | −1,72 | 0,086 | * | −0,86 | 0,395 | | −0,94 | 0,349 | | −1,45 | 0,150 | | −0,90 | 0,399 | |
| (−5; −1) | | | | | | | | | | | | | | | |
| CST | 0,05 | 0,522 | | −0,08 | 0,469 | | −0,10 | 0,460 | | 0,19 | 0,575 | | −0,32 | 0,373 | |
| CDT | 0,05 | 0,519 | | −0,05 | 0,480 | | −0,07 | 0,473 | | 0,11 | 0,543 | | −0,04 | 0,482 | |
| SCT | 0,05 | 0,522 | | −0,09 | 0,465 | | −0,07 | 0,472 | | 0,20 | 0,579 | | −0,31 | 0,378 | |
| MP | −1,37 | 0,171 | | 0,82 | 0,417 | | 0,91 | 0,365 | | −2,24 | 0,026 | ** | −1,13 | 0,297 | |
| MP corrected | −0,44 | 0,657 | | 0,27 | 0,787 | | 0,30 | 0,762 | | −0,72 | 0,473 | | −0,51 | 0,626 | |

(continued)

**Table 3.3** (continued)

| Event window | All GCO (abcd) (n = 233) | | | Disclaimer of opinion (c) (n = 59) | | | (bcd) (n = 70) | | | Emphasis of matter paragraph related to GC (a) (n = 163) | | | Except for (b) (n = 9) | | |
|---|---|---|---|---|---|---|---|---|---|---|---|---|---|---|---|
| | T | p-value | | T | p-value | | T | p-value | | T | p-value | | T | p-value | |
| **(+1; +5)** | | | | | | | | | | | | | | | |
| CST | −2,65 | 0,004 | *** | −2,45 | 0,007 | *** | −2,88 | 0,002 | *** | −0,98 | 0,163 | | −1,57 | 0,058 | * |
| CDT | −2,49 | 0,006 | *** | −1,50 | 0,067 | * | −1,86 | 0,031 | ** | −0,69 | 0,245 | | −0,27 | 0,393 | |
| SCT | −2,44 | 0,007 | *** | −2,35 | 0,009 | *** | −2,54 | 0,006 | *** | −0,91 | 0,181 | | −2,34 | 0,010 | *** |
| MP | −4,48 | 0,000 | *** | −3,29 | 0,002 | *** | −3,50 | 0,001 | *** | −3,07 | 0,003 | *** | −1,50 | 0,177 | |
| MP corrected | −2,57 | 0,011 | ** | −1,76 | 0,085 | * | −1,88 | 0,065 | * | −1,83 | 0,069 | * | −1,32 | 0,228 | |
| **(+5; +10)** | | | | | | | | | | | | | | | |
| CST | −0,37 | 0,357 | | −0,25 | 0,401 | | −0,70 | 0,241 | | 0,05 | 0,521 | | −1,15 | 0,125 | |
| CDT | −0,33 | 0,371 | | −0,13 | 0,449 | | −0,39 | 0,350 | | 0,04 | 0,515 | | −0,24 | 0,407 | |
| SCT | −0,35 | 0,364 | | −0,26 | 0,397 | | −0,60 | 0,275 | | 0,08 | 0,534 | | −1,22 | 0,112 | |
| MP | −1,82 | 0,070 | * | −0,59 | 0,558 | | −1,02 | 0,312 | | −1,51 | 0,133 | | −1,49 | 0,180 | |
| MP corrected | −1,02 | 0,308 | | −0,32 | 0,751 | | −0,56 | 0,578 | | −0,86 | 0,392 | | −1,04 | 0,334 | |
| **(+10; +15)** | | | | | | | | | | | | | | | |
| CST | −0,28 | 0,391 | | −1,04 | 0,149 | | −1,57 | 0,058 | * | 1,11 | 0,866 | | −2,14 | 0,016 | ** |
| CDT | −0,29 | 0,388 | | −0,74 | 0,231 | | −1,17 | 0,121 | | 0,80 | 0,788 | | −0,48 | 0,316 | |
| SCT | −0,30 | 0,383 | | −1,34 | 0,090 | * | −1,89 | 0,029 | ** | 1,17 | 0,878 | | −2,30 | 0,011 | ** |
| MP | −0,98 | 0,329 | | 0,16 | 0,871 | | −0,17 | 0,868 | | −1,06 | 0,291 | | −1,61 | 0,152 | |
| MP corrected | −0,55 | 0,582 | | 0,09 | 0,927 | | −0,09 | 0,929 | | −0,61 | 0,542 | | −0,83 | 0,432 | |

*Source* Author elaboration

*Notes* CST, Cross-sectional Test; CDT, Crude Dependence Test; SCT, Skewness Corrected test; MP, Mikkelson and Partch Test; MP corrected, Mikkelson and Partch Test with correction factor. Significant at: * 10, ** 5, *** 1%. (1) = emphasis of matter paragraph related to GCU; (2) = except for; (3) = disclaimer of opinion; (4) = adverse opinion

The CDT-test does not confirm the presence of pre-disclosure effects for all the different types of categories, since the statistics are never significant in the window [−15, −2).

In contrast, all other results are confirmed with the exception of post-announcement effects, measured in the window (+2, +15), for "disclaimer of opinion" and "except for". Moreover, it can be observed that the emphasis of matter paragraph related to GC does not have any impact on prices in (0; +1) and in (−1; +1).

The SCT-test confirms the results of the CST-test.

Overall, the MP-test confirms the results obtained using the CST-test in the windows [−15; +15], even if some differences emerge. In particular, there are no negative effects for "disclaimer of opinion". In contrast, with respect to "emphasis of matter paragraph related to GC", a negative post-announcement effect in the window (+2; +15) is shown. The last main difference is related to the pre-announcement effect of the "emphasis of matter paragraph related to GC" for which the MP test suggests a certain impact on returns in the windows (−10; −5) and (−5; −1), and a post-announcement effect in the window (+1; +5).

In applying the MP corrected test, no pre- and post-announcement effects are detected in the windows (−15; −2) and (+2; +15) for all the considered types of opinions. Furthermore, the introduction of the correction factor, $h$, contradicts the results in the window (−1; 0) for which the "all GCO" does not exhibit any effect on returns, as well as in (0; +1) for the "emphasis of matter paragraph related to GC". Switching the analysis to the windows closer to the audit report release, a negative impact for "all GCO" and "emphasis of matter paragraph related to GC" is confirmed. In more detail, the negative impact is verified at and around the event date (−1; +1).

Table 3.4 reports the results of the analysis referring to audit opinions, modified and unmodified, not containing an emphasis of matter paragraph related to GC. Afterwards, I separated the unmodified opinions with a generic emphasis of matter paragraph from the others in order to verify if, as expected, the emphasis of matter paragraph different from the GCO has a null or positive effect. In Table 3.4, I provide only the results for MP and MP corrected tests because the others are never statistically significant. This evidence is corroborated by the literature on ES (Castellano and Scaccia 2012; Castellano and D'Ecclesia 2013) in which it is argued that, on average, "positive" events or news have a weaker impact on stock returns than negative ones. Nevertheless, some interesting evidence was found.

Looking at unmodified opinions with a generic emphasis of matter paragraph, I found a strong positive pre-announcement effect on stock returns in the windows [−15; −2), [−15; −10) and (−5; −1) with reference to the MP test. On the other hand, I did not find any evidence of possible effects close to the event date and after. It is useful to highlight that the results provided by the MP corrected test are never statistically significant.

Finally, I provide the same tests considering all the opinions not containing a GCO. In this case the MP corrected test is statistically significant only in the window (−15; −2), detecting a positive impact on stock returns. Looking at the

**Table 3.4** Stock market's reaction to audit opinion—unmodified opinion and General emphasis of matter paragraph

| Event window | no GCO (n = 1204) | | | Emphasis of matter paragraph (generic) (n = 124) | | |
|---|---|---|---|---|---|---|
| | Z | p-value | | Z | p-value | |
| (−15; −2) | | | | | | |
| MP | 5,458 | 0,0000 | *** | 2,662 | 0,0088 | *** |
| MP corrected | 2,365 | 0,0182 | ** | 1,274 | 0,2051 | |
| (−2; +2) | | | | | | |
| MP | 3,236 | 0,0012 | *** | 1,732 | 0,0858 | |
| MP corrected | 1,469 | 0,1420 | | 0,960 | 0,3391 | |
| (+2; +15) | | | | | | |
| MP | 1,913 | 0,0560 | * | 1,155 | 0,2503 | |
| MP corrected | 0,876 | 0,3810 | | 0,629 | 0,5305 | |
| (0) | | | | | | |
| MP | 0,687 | 0,4923 | | 0,894 | 0,3733 | |
| MP corrected | 0,305 | 0,7608 | | 0,508 | 0,6122 | |
| (−1; 0) | | | | | | |
| MP | −0,179 | 0,8579 | | 1,008 | 0,3156 | |
| MP corrected | −0,081 | 0,9356 | | 0,572 | 0,5685 | |
| (0; +1) | | | | | | |
| MP | 1,750 | 0,0804 | * | 0,995 | 0,3216 | |
| MP corrected | 0,783 | 0,4335 | | 0,569 | 0,5703 | |
| (−1; +1) | | | | | | |
| MP | 1,096 | 0,2733 | | 1,090 | 0,2779 | |
| MP corrected | 0,499 | 0,6182 | | 0,604 | 0,5467 | |
| (−15; −10) | | | | | | |
| MP | 3,092 | 0,0020 | *** | 2,740 | 0,0071 | *** |
| MP corrected | 1,433 | 0,1521 | | 1,436 | 0,1536 | |
| (−10; −5) | | | | | | |
| MP | 2,117 | 0,0344 | ** | 1,123 | 0,2635 | |
| MP corrected | 0,973 | 0,3308 | | 0,654 | 0,5145 | |
| (−5; −1) | | | | | | |
| MP | 4,630 | 0,0000 | *** | 3,344 | 0,0011 | *** |
| MP corrected | 1,223 | 0,2214 | | 1,102 | 0,2727 | |
| (+1; +5) | | | | | | |
| MP | 1,718 | 0,0861 | * | 0,641 | 0,5226 | |
| MP corrected | 0,782 | 0,4346 | | 0,348 | 0,7283 | |

(continued)

**Table 3.4** (continued)

| Event window | no GCO (n = 1204) | | | Emphasis of matter paragraph (generic) (n = 124) | | |
|---|---|---|---|---|---|---|
| | Z | p-value | | Z | p-value | |
| (+5; +10) | | | | | | |
| MP | −0,061 | 0,9510 | | 1,458 | 0,1474 | |
| MP corrected | −0,028 | 0,9776 | | 0,868 | 0,3868 | |
| (+10; +15) | | | | | | |
| MP | 0,119 | 0,9055 | | −0,472 | 0,6374 | |
| MP corrected | 0,056 | 0,9557 | | −0,270 | 0,7878 | |

*Source* Author elaboration
*Notes* MP, Mikkelson and Partch Test; MP corrected, Mikkelson and Partch Test with correction factor. Significant at: $^{*}10$, $^{**}5$, $^{***}1\%$

MP-test, strong positive pre-announcement effects in the window $[-15; -2)$ can be observed. This result is also reinforced in all its sub-windows preceding the audit reports releases.

A weak positive post-announcement effect is also detected in the window (+2, +15], but this evidence is contradicted when looking at its sub-windows. Anyway, these results are not surprising, taking into consideration that the largest part of the sample is composed by pure clean opinion.

To my knowledge, it is clear that, at least for Italy, the issuance of a GCO is value relevant for investors, according to observed periods and used windows. The empirical evidence suggests that the debated effect is always negative even though we refer to unmodified opinion with an emphasis of matter paragraph related to GC. Ianniello and Galloppo (2015), in a prior period (2007–2010) obtain results contrasting with what I found. Hence, these results need to be empowered by further analysis in other countries and using bigger samples.

# References

Al-Thuneibat AA, Khamees BA, Al-Fayoumi NA (2008) The effect of qualified auditors' opinions on share prices: evidence from Jordan. Manag Audit J 23:84–101

Ameen EC, Chan K, Guffey DM (1994) Information content of qualified audit opinions for over-the-counter firms. J Bus Financ Account 21(7):997–1011

Baskin EF (1972) The communicative effectiveness of consistency exceptions. Account Rev 47:38–51

Boehmer E, Musumeci J, Poulsen A (1991) Event-study methodology under conditions of event-induced variance. J Financ Econ 30(2):253–272

Brown SJ, Warner JB (1980) Measuring security price performance. J Financ Econ 8:205–258

Brown SJ, Warner JB (1985) Using daily stock returns—the case of event studies. J Financ Econ 14:3–31

Campbell JY, Lo AW, MacKinlay AC (1997) Econometrics of financial markets. Princeton University Press, Princeton NJ

Carson E, Fargher NL, Geiger MA, Lennox CS, Raghunandan K, Willekens M (2013) Audit reporting for going-concern uncertainty: a research synthesis. Audit J Pract Theory 32(1):353–384. https://doi.org/10.2139/ssrn.2000496

Castellano R, D'Ecclesia RL (2013) CDS volatility: the key signal of credit quality. Ann Oper Res 205(1):89–107

Castellano R, Scaccia L (2012) CDS and rating announcements: changing signaling during the crisis? Rev Manag Sci 6(3):239–264

Chen KCW, Church KB (1996) Going concern opinions and the market's reaction to bankruptcy filings. Account Rev 71(1):117–128

Chow CW, Rice SJ (1982) Qualified audit opinions and share prices-an investigation. Audit J Pract Theory 1(2):35–53

Craswell AT (1985) Studies of the information content of qualified audit reports. J Bus Financ Account 12(1):93–115

Davis R (1982) An empirical evaluation of auditors "subject-to" opinions. Audit A J Pract Theory 2(1):13–32

Dodd P, Dopuch N, Holthausen R, Leftwich R (1984) Qualified audit opinions and stock prices. Information content, announcement dates, and concurrent disclosures. J Account Econ 6:3–38

Dopuch N, Hothausen R, Leftwich R (1986) Abnormal stock returns associated with media disclosure of subject to qualified audit opinions. J Account Econ 8:93–117

Elliott JA (1982) "Subject to" Audit opinions and abnormal security returns–outcomes and ambiguities. J Account Res 20:617–638

Fama EF (1991) Efficient capital markets: II. J. Finance 46(5):1575–1617

Firth M (1978) Qualified audit reports: their impact on investment decisions. Account Rev 53 (3):642–650

Holt G, Moizer P (1990) The meaning of audit reports. Account Bus Res 20(78):111–121

Ianniello G, Galloppo G (2015) Stock market reaction to auditor opinions—Italian evidence. Manag Audit J 30(6/7):610–632

Ittonen K (2012) Market reactions to qualified audit reports: research approaches. Account Res J 25(1):8–24

Kolari JW, Pynnönen S (2010) Event study testing with cross-sectional correlation of abnormal returns. Rev Financ Stud 23(11):3996–4025

Mentz M, Schiereck D (2008) Cross-border mergers and the cross-border effect: the case of the automotive supply industry. Rev Manag Sci 2(3):199–218

Mikkelson WH, Partch MM (1988) Withdrawn security offerings. J Financ Quant Anal 23(2):119–133

Ogneva M, Subramanyam KR (2007) Does the stock market underreact to going concern opinions? evidence from the U.S. and Australia. J Account Econ 43(2–3):439–452

Pucheta-Martínez MC, Martínez AV, Benau MAG (2004) Reactions of the Spanish capital market to qualified audit reports. Eur Account Rev 13(4):689–711

Soltani B (2000) Some empirical evidence to support the relationship between audit reports and stock prices—the French case. Int J Audit 4(3):269–291. https://doi.org/10.1111/1099-1123.00317

Taffler RJ, Lu J, Kausar A (2004) In denial? Stock market underreaction to going-concern audit report disclosures. J Account Econ 38:263–296

Tahinakis P, Samarinas M (2016) The incremental information content of audit opinion. J Appl Account Res 17(2):139–169

# Chapter 4
# Audit Reporting for Going Concern Uncertainty: Literature Insights, Italian Evidence and Future Research Approaches and Pathways

**Abstract** This chapter provides the main findings reached from the journey through Audit Reporting for GCU. First of all, it résumés the main insights retrieved from the narrative literature review performed in Chap. 2; secondly, it contextualizes the results achieved in the empirical study (Chap. 3) conducted regarding the consequences on investors in Italy, also in Chap. 3; lastly, it outlines future trajectories for: scholars, suggesting future pathways of research and stressing the importance to "glocalize" results achieved, especially in archival studies; regulators, asking for a fine tuning action of current standards in accordance with the evidence provided throughout this study; auditors, calling for fair opinions more than in the past in the light of new standard requirements and to prevent other financial crises and/or scandals; investors, demanding a higher awareness about the deep meaning of a GCO, especially after novelties occurred that have rendered a GCO close to being mandatory, as seen in Chap. 1.

## 4.1 Insights from the Worldwide Literature

Recent years' global financial crises have moved the public attention to the pivotal role played by public companies in influencing the global economic sector, either directly or indirectly. The need for a fine-tuning regulation has clearly arisen in all sectors, especially regarding the internal and external controls of firms' performance and financial health, with the aim of preventing additional problems and to foster a speedy recovery (Jones 2011; Kvaal and Nobes 2012; Lev and Gu 2016; Sercu et al. 2006).

As regards the external auditing process, the auditor of a client firm takes on the responsibility of assessing its ability to continue as a GC for approximately a one year period. Even if the auditor's assessment does not have to be foolproof by nature, his or her judgement can be a determinant for the future of the organization being audited. These concerns have traditionally been present in the American and European cultural regimes.

S. Brunelli, *Audit Reporting for Going Concern Uncertainty*, SpringerBriefs in Accounting, https://doi.org/10.1007/978-3-319-73046-2_4

The narrative literature review on audit reporting for GCU undertaken in Chap. 2 has created an overall framework within which it is possible to reflect upon the factors influencing GCOs.

At first glance, what emerges is that the issuance of a GCO covers a fundamental, informational role for present and future shareholders, even though only a moderate number of stakeholder centred studies have been detected.

With respect to the determinants of GCOs, the essential role of auditors' judgement on all the other factors that can influence the auditor's decision clearly emerges. Not only the experience possessed by the auditor, but also the size of the audit firm for which he or she works can influence the degree of independence maintained during the audit service relationship.

The same can be asserted for the accuracy of the issuance of GCOs for subsequently failing or not failing firms: in fact, the evidence gathered from different scholars confirms that it is possible for stakeholders to trust the opinions issued by Big 4 firms (because of their unequivocal strong power) more than the ones by non-Big 4 firms.

Regarding the consequences of GCOs, stock prices usually change according to the expectations investors have of firms' performance. The information provided by GCOs to the market cause it to produce abnormal security returns, especially for GCOs' first issuance. From the lenders' point of view, especially in the USA, and as was expected, the issuance of a GCO is quite likely to cause a downgrading of a firm's credit rating, with negative consequences on the possibilities of financing access.

Furthermore, PCAOB is considering the possibility of harmonizing its auditing standard related to GCOs with the ISA 570 revised. Recently, it has published Staff Audit Practice Alert No.13 of 2014, which declares their intention to review AU sec. 341 and evaluate potential revisions to that auditing standard, including consideration of accounting standards and input from the Board's advisory groups. Finally, Standard-Setting Updates have fixed the timing of the process of the PCAOB agenda. Among the different projects, GC discussion and revision is proposed as the next action under consideration for 2018.

This fact can be interpreted as a sign of the importance of further analyzing GCOs among the three main categories individuated by Carson et al. (2013).

## 4.2   Evidence from Italy: Consequences' Implications

Summing up the results of the analysis performed in Chap. 3, I notice that investor' perceptions change suddenly and vary over time. In the period from 2008-2014, a GCO was seen as something negative because ISA 570 and 700 in their old versions required the stressing of GC uncertainty only when possible doubts arose during the auditing process. Now that a GC paragraph is close to being "mandatory", even when there are no doubts about the foreseeable future of the firm, I expect that investors are able to capture the difference and, in turn, a mixed stock returns reaction may result in the future. In addition, some reflections emerge when considering the main features of the Italian listed firms' accounting system, market environment and corporate governance mechanisms. As already known, according to Nobes (1998), the Italian accounting system is encompassed in culture type II where the primary users of financial statements are government and creditors. This evidence feeds the debate on corporate governance mechanisms (Cremers and Nair 2005) and represents one of the main reasons that modify the traditional agency problem, placing Italian firms among those with agency problems of type II (Di Pietra et al. 2008). Thus, conflicts exist between majority and minority shareholders, rather than shareholders and managers (agency problems of type I). For this reason, it is possible that auditors' independence is undermined by the power of majority shareholders from the time of the auditor appointment process. This could represent a theoretical explanation of the empirical evidence found in Chap. 3. Minority shareholders do not trust with the auditor independence. Hence, whatever the degree of severity of an opinion, minority shareholders perceive negatively the presence of a GCO, especially during a financial crisis.

Past researches have suggested different solutions for minimizing agency problem type II, such as: an increase of non-executive and/or independent directors (Barontini and Bozzi 2011; Core et al. 2006; Fama and Jensen 1983; Ianniello 2015) and different financial and non-financial incentive systems for managers (Ye 2014; Pott et al. 2014). Most of the time these "remedies" have failed to solve problems and conflicts. For these reasons, my advice is to work towards an information dissemination process among investors of the auditing standard changes related to the ISAs' revision. This could be effective, especially in Italy, where the majority of the firms are SMEs and family-owned and most of the time the minority shareholders are naïve and inexperienced investors. Otherwise, the riskiness of a continuously negative stock market reaction, due to GCOs, whatever the real financial health of the audited firm, may not be negligible with negative reflections on the entire economy.

Finally, it seems possible to outline the implications of the research for:

- investors: the need for an information dissemination process aimed at explaining in depth the different mean of positive and negative GCOs, since its almost obligatory paragraph for periods ending on or after 15th December, 2016, is stressed;
- regulators: the IAASB should take into account that in several jurisdictions, such as Italy, the GCO is negatively perceived, even when it is a related paragraph within a clean opinion; if so, a further fine-tuning of ISAs related to GCOs could be provided by taking into account the "two" type II problems recalled with regard to accounting system and agency theory academic insights. The PCAOB should consider the possibility of making different amendments during the convergence process in order to take into account the different problems deriving from a different market environment, such as in the USA.
- auditors: as financial scandals and frauds have demonstrated throughout the world, most of the time severe opinions were not given at all or given too late,

when the minority investors would no longer be able to avoid heavy damages. Where some doubts arose during the auditing process the answer provided by auditors has been the release of an unmodified opinion with an emphasis of matter paragraph related to GC rather than a severe opinion. Now that the GCO is close to being mandatory, auditors may strive to enhance, as best they can, the value relevance of GCOs for investors.

## 4.3  Audit Reporting for GCOs: Future Pathways Approaches to the Issue

Generally, studies related to audit reporting for GCU are undertaken in one or several countries where scholars gathered data. As we have seen, especially among the archival studies, research questions are most of the time aimed at detecting one or more features included in the academic debate reviewed in Chap. 2. What I detected most of the time in my review is the continuous attempt by scholars to generalize results for a continent or even worldwide, without taking into account the important differences that characterize the market environment in which studies are performed. My criticism does not refer to the well known differences in terms of accounting and auditing standards and practices (Hatfield 1911; Nobes 1998, 2006; Kvaal and Nobes 2010). Rather, the focal point is represented by the way in which the agency problem has its characterization worldwide. As highlighted by many scholars, three (main) types of agency problem:

1. Type 1: the classic agency problems, according to pioneeristic studies in the field, between owners and managers that are in conflict, mainly, in decision making process related to which and how strategies should be pursued. Essentially, the issue of how shareholders can control the management actions arises. This problem is particularly felt for public companies;
2. Type 2: the agency problem deriving from concentrated ownership. Concentrated ownership refers to the situation where there is the presence of an owner with a large block of shares or an owner of several large blocks of shares in the firm. This could undermine minority investors' rights and the ability to control managers' behaviours (that are totally in the hands of the majority shareholder(s));
3. Type 3: especially in contexts where the profit maximization still represents a "Mantra", shareholders (both minority and majority ones) may put in action biased cognitive behaviours detrimental for the the remaining stakeholder population. An example is the suddenly stopped of an operating plant in areas where it is hard that the employees will be able to find other employment, or the decision to implement risky strategies damaging the possibility to repay debts as they mature and, more in general, in all cases where a misalignment between shareholders' interests (often represented by simple profit maximization) and stakeholder interests emerges.

If on the one hand the study's "localization" has gathered ground over time, in particular for archival studies, where the efforts made to gather data are great and the time to conclude a research is short, on the other hand, remarks and conclusions, of the main part of reviewed studies, have tried to suggest universal solutions by pursuing a study of "globalization". In this sense it is not helpful to find articles where a researcher, after a series of statements and restrictions, generalize his/her conclusions. Rather what seems more honest, and something that I wish for future research pathways, is to avoid an excess of simplification that, in the end, is *per se* detrimental to the results reached.

In brief, the "glocalization" of studies on Audit Reporting for GCU, based on the nature and types of agency problems, could represent a good driver and an effective answer to the question posed by Carson et al. (2013): *"How do factors such us culture and societal pressures affect auditors' GCO-related decision?"*

In their popular article, Carson et al. (2013) concluded with a series of open issues aimed at fostering future researches on audit reporting for GCU. Their issues seemed like seeds on the grass claiming water from scholars. Briefly, they asked for an in-depth engagement from scholars related to:

- Qualitative studies to better describe auditor-client interaction as there are a huge number of quantitative researches with very different conclusions and suggestions;
- Studies aimed at analyzing GCOs' effects in financial institutions because of the greater risk of a systematic crisis, given the role of banks in the economy;
- Studies for Non-Profit and Governmental entities because of the few numbers of extant studies;
- Study replications over time about error type I and II misclassifications because of their intrinsic usefulness in understanding firms' market dynamics in different environments;
- Researches about the consequences of GCOs for financial analysts and other market participants, because the great number of existing studies, included those I provide in Chap. 3, mainly refer to the consequences for current or potential shareholders;
- Studies concerning the responsibility for Going Concern Disclosures to better distinguish between management, audit committee and auditor roles around GCU;
- A paradigm change in terms of research methods and approaches. In particular these should encourage the adoption of experimental studies in place of archival ones. In Carlson et al.'s opinion the latter are better at investigating the GCO decision-making process. This is an underexplored field by scholars.

Four years on, not many things have changed except for studies about the responsibility for GC disclosure. As is known, the novelty has been the revision of several ISAs (570 above all) that has increased auditor responsibility and disclosures in checking GC appropriateness and that definitely gave management the responsibility for being in charge of it.

Indeed, the remaining Carson et al. (2013) issues are still totally or partially open. In my view other additional research pathways could be:

- Further studies on GC disclosures because of the referenced ISAs' revision and the possible convergence of US GAAS (as demonstrated by recent PCAOB research setting agenda updates);
- Studies located in countries where the agency problem type II is felt, aimed at detecting if and in which manner auditors are more or less in favour, than in other jurisdictions, of issuing a GCO, given they (by definition) have more dependence from majority shareholders;
- An increase of studies located in the rest of the world, especially in emerging and developing economies, because of the scarce numbers of studies and the low reliability that they have most of the time;
- Policy papers aimed at suggesting how better to regulate important aspects, such as the GCO issuance, of the auditing profession in developing countries.

Lastly, I was impressed by the huge lack, especially in the USA, in investigating consequences of GCOs for other stakeholders than shareholders and lenders. How react suppliers, customers, managers and other employees to GCOs? As regard, an interesting study was recently conducted by Amin and Harris (2017) in non profit organizations. Thus, studies on this line are encouraged both for corporation (listed and non listed) and partnership. Using mainly quantitative methods for the former and case studies and/or experimental studies for the latter.

# References

Amin K, Harris EE (2017) Nonprofit stakeholder response to going-concern audit opinions. 1303 J Account Audit Finan 32(3):329–349

Barontini R, Bozzi S (2011) Board compensation and ownership structure: empirical evidence for Italian listed companies. J Manag Gov 15:59–89

Carson E, Fargher NL, Geiger MA, Lennox CS, Raghunandan K, Willekens M (2013) Audit reporting for going-concern uncertainty: a research synthesis. Audit J Pract Theory 32(1):353–384. https://doi.org/10.2139/ssrn.2000496

Core JE, Guay WR, Rusticus TO (2006) Does weak governance cause weak stock returns? An examination of firm operating performance and investors' expectations. J Finance 61(2):655–687. https://doi.org/10.1111/j.1540-6261.2006.00851.x

Cremers M, Nair V (2005) Governance mechanisms and equity prices. J Finance 60(6):2859–2894

Di Pietra R, Grambovas C, Raonic V, Riccaboni A (2008) The effects of board size and 'busy' directors on the market value of Italian companies. J Manag Gov 12(1):73–91. https://doi.org/10.1007/s10997-008-9044-y

Fama EF, Jensen MC (1983) Separation of ownership and control. J Law Econ 26(2):301–325

Hatfield HR (1911) Some variations in accounting practice in England, France, Germany and the United States. J Account Res 4(2):169–182

Ianniello G (2015) The effects of board and auditor independence on earnings quality: evidence from Italy. J Manag Gov 19:229–253. https://doi.org/10.1007/s10997-013-9285-2

Jones MJ (2011) Creative accounting, fraud and international accounting scandals. Wiley, Chichester

Kvaal E, Nobes CW (2010) international differences in IFRS policy choice: a research note. Account Bus Res 40(2):173–187

Kvaal E, Nobes CW (2012) IFRS policy changes and the continuation of national patterns of ifrs practice. Eur Account Rev 21(2):343–371

Lev B, Gu F (2016) The end of accounting and the path forward for investors and managers. Wiley, New York

Nobes C (1998) Towards a general model of the reasons for international differences in financial reporting. ABACUS 34(2):162–187

Nobes C (2006) The survival of international differences under IFRS: towards a research agenda. Account Bus Res 36(3):233–245

Pott C, Tebben T, Watrin C (2014) The effect of outside directors' and auditors' incentives on managers' ability to manage cash bonuses. J Manag Gov 18(3):505–540

Sercu P, Vander Bauwhede H, Willekens M (2006) Post-Enron implicit audit reporting standards: sifting through the evidence. Economist 154(3):389–403. https://doi.org/10.1007/s10645-006-9016-z

Ye K (2014) Independent director cash compensation and earning management. J Account Public Policy 33:391–400

Printed by Printforce, the Netherlands